At greatest risk

The children most likely to be poor

Edited by
Gabrielle Preston

CPAG
94 White
London

CPAG is the leading charity campaigning for the abolition of poverty among children and young people in the UK and for the improvement of the lives of low-income families. CPAG aims to: raise awareness of the extent, nature and impact of poverty; bring about positive income policy changes for families with children in poverty; and enable those eligible for benefits and tax credits to have access to their full entitlement. If you are not already supporting us, please consider making a donation or ask for details of our membership schemes and publications.

Poverty Publication 113

Published by Child Poverty Action Group
94 White Lion Street, London N1 9PF

Registered Company No.1993854
Charity No.294841

© Child Poverty Action Group 2005

ISBN 1 901698 78 5

Cover and design by Devious Designs 0114 275 5634
Typeset by Boldface 020 7833 8868
Printed by Russell Press 0115 978 4505
Cover photo: www.JohnBirdsall.co.uk. Library photo posed by models.

Contents

Acknowledgements

I am very grateful to all the people who contributed to this book. Particular thanks are due to Ruth Lister and David Piachaud for their support with planning the book, and their helpful comments, and to Paul Dornan, Kate Green and Gary Craig for reading and commenting on the draft version. I am particularly grateful to Pauline Phillips at CPAG for editing and managing the production of this book. Many thanks also to Rowena Mayhew for proofreading the text.

About the authors

Jonathan Bradshaw is Professor of Social Policy at the University of York.

Sarah Cemlyn is Senior Lecturer in the School for Policy Studies, University of Bristol.

Colin Clark is Senior Lecturer in Sociology in the Department of Geography and Sociology at the University of Strathclyde, Glasgow.

Gary Craig is Professor of Social Justice at the University of Hull.

Paul Dornan is Head of Policy and Research at CPAG.

Pamela Fitzpatrick is a welfare rights worker at CPAG.

Ruth Lister is Professor of Social Policy, Loughborough University, and Donald Dewar Visiting Professor of Social Justice, University of Glasgow.

Peter McCarthy is Honorary Principal Research Associate at the Newcastle Centre for Family Studies.

Sue Middleton is Director of the Centre for Research and Social Policy, Department of Social Studies, Loughborough University.

Jenny Neuburger is Senior Policy Officer at Shelter.

Ruth Northway is Professor of Learning Disability Nursing at the Unit for Development in Intellectual Disabilities, School of Care Sciences, University of Glamorgan.

Richard Olsen is a Research Fellow in the Nuffield Community Care Studies Unit at the University of Leicester.

David Piachaud is Professor of Social Policy at the London School of Economics.

Gabrielle Preston is Policy and Research Officer at CPAG.

Sue Regan is Director of Policy at Shelter.

Mike Stein is Director of the Social Work Research and Development Unit at the University of York.

Hugh Stickland is an Economic Adviser at the Department for Work and Pensions.

Janet Walker is Professor of Family Policy and Director of the Newcastle Centre for Family Studies at the University of Newcastle upon Tyne.

Foreword

The scale of child poverty in this country, even after the gradual reduction of recent years, shames us all. The particular plight of some of the most disadvantaged children is, as David Piachaud argues in this book, a responsibility that we all share.

Children are frequently seen as a homogeneous, undifferentiated group because they constitute a category in their own right. As a sub-category of children, children living in poverty are even more likely to be thought of as a single group. This new report from CPAG is unusual in that it focuses in depth on particular groups of children living in poverty or at risk of poverty. These groups are not all discrete, as there are degrees of overlap between them. Nevertheless, by separating them out for analysis, the report deepens our understanding of child poverty and helps to point to where policies need to be strengthened.

In some cases the greater risk of poverty is associated with the characteristics or situation of the child alone, for instance disabled children or children leaving care; in others it is associated with the characteristics or situation of the parent(s) alone, such as imprisonment or, again, disability. In contrast, child poverty in larger families is connected to a characteristic of the family itself. In the case of black and minority ethnic (BME) children, Gypsies and Travellers and asylum seekers, the minority status of the family as a whole is implicated in the children's poverty. Finally, as Sue Regan and Jenny Neuburger point out, the common characteristic of children in acute housing need is the structural problem of their housing need. Ultimately, though, whatever the immediate individual or family-linked causal factors, we have to look for underlying structural factors to understand why, for instance, disability or BME status are associated with a higher risk of child poverty.

Some of the groups identified in this report – such as disabled children and BME children – do figure in official statistics and some conventional poverty analyses. However, even in such cases, a number of chapters point to the inadequacies of official data or of the research evidence. Other groups, such as care-leavers and children living in Gypsy and Traveller families or asylum seeking families, are simply invisible in the poverty statistics and in most poverty analysis. Yet the evidence presented here suggests that they are particularly vulnerable to poverty and to different forms of social exclusion.

A theme common to a number of chapters is one to which CPAG has drawn attention over many years: the inadequacy of benefit rates for families not in paid work. The New Labour Government, in its first two terms of office, has done much more to address this issue than it promised on coming to power. Nevertheless, in understandably prioritising children's benefit rates, it has ignored those of their parents. Yet, as many contributors point out, the overall adequacy of benefits for children depend on the rates paid to parents as well as children. This is a point also underlined in a recent Women's Budget Group report on the links between women's poverty and child poverty.[1]

Poverty affects children's psychological as well as material wellbeing, as brought out by Mike Stein's contribution in particular. Children in poverty generally are all too often treated as 'different' from other children and as 'other'.[2] Children in some of the groups discussed in this report also face the prejudices all too often associated with racism or disablism. Children in demonised minority groups – notably asylum seekers and Gypsy and Traveller families – are even more likely to be Othered. This is an aspect of poverty which tends to be underplayed in government documents on poverty. However, the Welsh Assembly Government pays it more attention in its child poverty strategy, one of the aims of which is 'to remove the myths and stigma attached to poverty'.[3] The Welsh Assembly Government also emphasises the need to address participation poverty and to listen to and treat all children with respect. Participation and voice are issues raised in this report, in particular by Sarah Cemlyn and Colin Clark in their chapter on the social exclusion of Gypsy and Traveller children, by Jan Walker and Peter McCarthy in their analysis of children with parents in prison, and by Pamela Fitzpatrick in her chapter on asylum seekers.

A focus on specific groups of children at greatest risk of poverty offers some policy signposts for the re-elected Labour Government, if the target of eradicating child poverty is ever to be achieved. Some of these point to strengthening policies that support families with children generally: for instance, further real increases in child benefit and greater investment in social housing. Others indicate where policy may need to be better attuned to particular needs: for instance, those of larger families or asylum seeking families. Moreover, given the emphasis now placed on monitoring, indicators need to be developed in order better to monitor progress in reducing poverty and social exclusion among children at greatest risk of poverty.

Some of the problems faced by the various groups of children who experience poverty and social exclusion are common across the groups and some are particular to individual groups. They combine to jeopardise the well-being of children and their chances of living a flourishing life both as children in the here and now and as adults in the future. I hope that this report will help to draw public attention to the urgent need to ensure that all children genuinely share in the opportunity promised by politicians.

Ruth Lister
Professor of Social Policy, Loughborough University, and Donald Dewar Visiting Professor of Social Justice, University of Glasgow

Notes

1 WBG, *Women's and Children's Poverty: making the links*, Women's Budget Group, 2005
2 R Lister, *Poverty*, Polity Press, 2004
3 Welsh Assembly Government, *A Fair Future for Our Children: The Strategy of the Welsh Assembly Government for Tackling Child Poverty*, Welsh Assembly Government, 2005, p4

Introduction
Gabrielle Preston

The Government's commitment on the reduction of global poverty and the high profile *Make Poverty History* campaign have left us in little doubt that poverty matters – and apparently people care about it. Why, then, did poverty slip right off the political agenda during the recent general election? A vituperative campaign that focused on the war in Iraq and sought to appeal to the baser instincts of middle England – particularly around immigration – did little to illuminate a social and political agenda for a new Government or illustrate the progress made by previous administrations in the wake of New Labour's pledge to eradicate child poverty. With both Labour and Conservatives trumpeting the virtues of 'hard working families' it is hardly surprising that families who are out of work, for whatever reason, feel both marginalised and stigmatised.

It is disheartening but perhaps not surprising that during the election campaign the Government was relatively mute about child poverty in the UK, and its many bold initiatives to reduce it. We are, as David Piachaud points out in Chapter 1, somewhat selective about which particular aspects of poverty engender guilt and concern. Although poverty in the Third World – for which we may or may not feel responsible – often arouses our outrage and compassion and, in times of particular crisis, sometimes even our generosity, we are less inclined to accept its existence at home. We are, it seems, more preoccupied with poverty in Africa than with black children living in poverty in the UK.[1]

Despite this national myopia, in the wake of the Prime Minister Tony Blair's bold commitment to 'end child poverty for ever'[2] progress has been made in many areas. The Government accepts that poverty is a multifaceted phenomenon and has introduced a range of initiatives designed to deal with it. These include improvements in financial support for children via child tax credit and child benefit, the introduction of working tax credit and the minimum wage to help low paid earners, along with the Sure Start initiative and the ten-year strategy for childcare, designed to support children and help parents – primarily lone parents – into work. These policy initiatives have made a real change to a great many children's lives, proving that poverty and disadvantage are not just an unfortunate fact of life but are issues that – with the political will – can be addressed. However, more needs to be done to consolidate the progress made and ensure that every child truly does have 'the best start in life'.[3]

Although the Government has become expert at explaining the sort of problems children face,[4] further action is clearly needed to translate welcome rhetoric into more effective action. We urge the new Government to take note of the powerful messages to emerge from this book, and to incorporate the specific and general recommendations into the forthcoming Spending Review.

Winners and losers

At Greatest Risk reveals that, although some children have benefited from government initiatives, not all children have benefited equally. Ironically – or tragically – as progress is made, children who are most at risk of poverty are being left behind. These children are not just falling behind an increasingly prosperous population (in which disparities between the richest and the poorest sectors remain unacceptably large), they are falling behind other children living in low income households who have benefited from the welfare to work focus of government policy. The children under discussion in this book – who need to get more to overcome multiple disadvantages – are getting less. Why are these children failing to gain equally – let alone disproportionately, as they should – from policies put in place by a Government that is intent on eradicating poverty?

At greatest risk?

It is widely accepted that some children are at greater risk of poverty than others. The proportion of children living in poverty in two-parent households ranges from 3 per cent where both parents are in full-time work to 77 per cent where neither parent is employed. Children in lone-parent families are twice as likely to live in poverty as those in couple families. Children in Pakistani/Bangladeshi households are by far the most likely to live in poverty – apart, perhaps from asylum seekers, whose economic status is not recorded in income poverty statistics.

However, although poverty is very well documented, this book reveals a shocking paucity of statistical information about many of the families and children under discussion. Despite the accumulation of a mass of data under the Labour Government, statistical information does not reveal the real incidence of poverty within some of these groups, let alone capture the degree to which children span some, or all, of the 'at risk' groups. *At Greatest Risk* also exposes the inability of current statistical data to capture and present the reality of poverty for many children. Given the amount of data generated by the Department for Work and Pensions, Inland Revenue, the Department of Health and the Department for Education and Skills, together with the devolved administrations, the inadequacies and gaps in statistical information about children who are most at risk are hard to understand. Despite exhaustive school and health records, some of the children who are at greatest risk of living in poverty appear to be largely invisible. Where statistics do exist, they may distort or underestimate the numbers involved.

A number of other themes thread their way through each of the chapters in this book. Tragically, in the 21st century, women and children continue to be at greatest risk of living in poverty. Disgracefully, a person's ethnic origin is still closely associated with inadequate educational and income levels. It is clear that whatever the particular characteristics of a household that place a child at risk of poverty – be they disability, worklessness and/or lone parenthood – underlying disadvantage is greatly compounded the more 'at risk' groups a child falls into.

How this book is organised

At Greatest Risk considers the particular issues and experiences faced by children from disadvantaged groups, drawing parallels where appropriate. Why are these children losing out? Are there structural problems – for example, anomalies within the tax credit, benefit, education or employment systems – or are families failing to access support that is available because of lack of information, problems with access or discrimination? Are targeted interventions indicated, or do current forms of universal support need to be improved? Why are so many children failing to gain the qualifications they need to access rewarding, and well remunerated, employment? Is reducing unemployment the answer, or should more attention be paid to benefit adequacy?

Part 1 outlines the wider poverty context and considers the extent, causes and consequences of poverty. Part 2 considers different groups of children who are most at risk of poverty. Although the chapter titles suggest that these are discrete and largely homogenous, significant numbers of children span different – some perhaps all – of these groups. A number of depressingly familiar themes thread their way through each and every chapter, linking families and children from, and within, the different groups. Whether a child is from a black minority ethnic group, has just left care, has a disabled parent, is sick or disabled – or in some cases, all four – all of the children in *At Greatest Risk* share stark childhood experiences and bleak prospects for the future.

Various definitions of poverty are used in *At Greatest Risk*. Most contributors cite 60 per cent of median income as the poverty line. Townsend's definition of relative poverty is also used.[5] The authors use various measures and indicators, partly because they are reliant upon the often woefully inadequate data that is available, and partly to illuminate differing aspects of poverty and social exclusion. As this book reveals, there are immense variations of poverty, whether families are income poor or not. The fundamental issue of income poverty is linked with other factors that limit families' resources – including educational and housing inequalities, ineffective or inaccessible public services, poor health, low skills and inadequate access to the labour market.

An historic third term?

Labour has now won a third term in power and is in a position to address some of the issues raised in this book. The majority of British voters placed social policy issues – the welfare state, education and health – at the centre of their political concerns. The results suggest that the Government should perhaps be a tad less cautious about treading on the toes of middle England. Where anxieties are inflamed by a bigoted and ill-informed media, particularly with regard to asylum seekers, the Government needs to grasp the initiative and introduce policies that complement and do not detract from its overall strategy on child poverty. Instead of trying to prove that it can be as harsh – indeed, harsher – than other political parties, it should inform the British people of the economic, social and moral advantages of supporting all children living in the UK, irrespective of their parents' status.[6]

For the moment, progress on child poverty appears to be faltering. It is unclear whether the Government will attain its interim target of reducing child poverty by a quarter by 2005, let alone halve it by 2010, with its current policies. More energy needs to be channelled into addressing the primary causes of poverty – low income due to an inadequate benefit system or low pay – and less time spent punishing some of its consequences – often ill health, worklessness and social alienation. Reform of incapacity benefit must be handled with sensitivity and care. Early interventions are more effective – and economic – than punitive retrospective action. It is neither ethical nor economic to punish children because of their parents' status, or because systemic failures have rendered them vulnerable.

It is neither fair nor just that the most vulnerable children, who need additional support to compensate them for the multiple disadvantages they suffer, should receive less because of their parents' status as 'workless', as prisoners or as asylum seekers. Policy initiatives are urgently needed to ensure that the UK can deal more humanely and effectively with the most vulnerable people in our society. They must reflect – and inform – public aspirations for a society that is significantly more egalitarian than is currently in evidence.

This book contains a clear message for the new Government. Child poverty is extremely costly. In the short term, lack of financial support renders people's lives on average shorter and childhoods more brutal than those of their better-off peer group. In the long term, poverty not only blights lives, it exacts a huge cost on both individuals and society in terms of ill health or disability, lower educational attainment levels, inadequate access to training, and significantly poorer long-term chances of reasonably paid, sustainable employment.

If the Government really wants this to be an historic third term, it must be bolder in both presenting and developing policies to reduce social and financial inequality in this country. If *all* children are to be given the best start in life, the Government must accept that, although the emphasis on work during its first and second term has helped some children move out of poverty, it has failed to reduce significant inequalities at the lower end of the income scale. Security really must be provided to children whose parents are not in paid employment. It is not sufficient to legislate to the advantage of some children all of the time, or for all children some of the time. The Government must aim to support all children all of the time, but ensure that those who are most at risk of poverty benefit the most.

Notes

1   See WBG, *Women's and Children's Poverty: making the links, Women's Budget Group*, 2005, available at www.wbg.org.uk

2   Tony Blair's speech at Toynbee Hall, reproduced in R Walker (ed), *Ending Child Poverty: popular welfare in the 21st century?*, Policy Press, 1999

3   A term utilised in a number of Government documents, including HM Treasury, DfES, DWP, DTI, *Choice for Parents, the Best Start for Children: a ten year strategy for childcare*, HMSO, December 2004

4   See, for example, HM Treasury, *Child Poverty Review*, The Stationery Office, 2004; Social Exclusion Unit, *Breaking the Cycle: taking stock of progress and priorities for the future*, Office of the Deputy Prime Minister, 2004; Department for Education and Skills, *Every Child Matters*, Consultation Paper, Cm 5860, The Stationery Office, 2003; Department for Education and Skills, *Every Child Matters: Change for Children*, The Stationery Office, 2004; Prime Minister's Strategy Unit (jointly with DWP, DoH, DfES, ODPM), *Improving the Life Chances of Disabled People: Final report*, January 2005

5   'People are relatively deprived if they cannot obtain, at all or sufficiently, the conditions of life – that is, the diets, amenities, standards and services – which allow them to play the roles, participate in the relationships and follow the customary behaviour which is expected of them by virtue of their membership of society', Peter Towsend, *Poverty in the United Kingdom*, Penguin, 1979, p31

6   See P Toynbee, 'Unlike Zeta Jones', *The Guardian*, 2 March 2005, in which she discusses the findings from *Life Chances: What do the public really think about poverty?* published by the Fabian Society in 2005, and concludes that 'When you actually talk to real voters about beating poverty, they get quite excited. So why doesn't Labour do it?'

Part one

Poverty trends: causes and consequences of poverty

One
Child poverty: an overview
David Piachaud

Introduction

Children are one-fifth of Britain's population and all our future, as Gordon Brown frequently points out. The circumstances in which children live, the opportunities they have, the influences on them for good and bad all shape their experiences while a child, their lives as adults and, in turn, generations as yet unborn. Parents are responsible for a child's existence and in large part for a child's upbringing but society has a responsibility and concern with the welfare of all children.

Every child whose life is blighted by poverty is an individual whose hopes, opportunities and happiness are constricted, constrained and curtailed. If this were inevitable it would be a sad fact we had to live with. Since it is not inevitable it remains a national and a global disgrace.

Yet there is a tendency to pass by on the other side of the street. Britain is a prosperous country and we are all going forward, not back. In comparison with the past, poverty has ceased to exist. All the poor have colour televisions, most have mobile phones and many have money to burn in the form of cigarettes – how then can you talk of poverty? Poverty worldwide is sad but we cannot do much about it. It is a product of civil wars and corruption plus natural disasters – to which we respond most charitably if they figure prominently on television.

Sadly, the effects of such attitudes – dismissing child poverty as no longer a problem or as beyond our control or our concern – are the same. It ceases to be a challenge, an offence to any notion of civilisation and something about which action must be taken.

In the face of such attitudes, the grounds for concern about child poverty must be re-stated, its causes re-examined, its inevitability questioned, its solutions explored. This is what this book sets out to do.

Poverty, like disease, ultimately affects individuals' lives, each one of which is different. To understand what is happening, however, we cannot simply rely on individual histories. We must look more broadly. In this chapter, the evidence about child poverty in Britain as a whole is reviewed. In later chapters, poverty among different groups is described and analysed; these groups are part of British society but they differ in important respects in terms of the extent and the impact of child poverty, in the causes of poverty and in the appropriateness and effectiveness of policies to tackle poverty.

It is beyond the scope of this book to examine child poverty on a global scale. But it is important to remember that, while the extent of poverty differs in degree, its effects are similar in nature. The latest UNICEF report, *The State of the World's Children*,[1] sets out for 2003 the stark contrast between children's lives in developing countries, where most of the world's children live, and in industrialised countries.

	Developing countries	Industrialised countries
Gross national income per head	US$1,300	US$28,000
Life expectancy at birth	62 years	78 years
Enrolment in primary schools	78%	96%
Infant mortality rate	6%	0.5%

Within Britain there are also stark differences.

	Bottom	Top
Income (deciles)[2]	£170	£660
Life expectancy (local authorities)[3]	69.1 years	80.1 years
Poor education (social class)[4]	77%	32%

Imagine if you were suddenly told you would lose 11 years of your life or were deprived of a decent education, putting not only this book but whole tracts of modern living beyond your comprehension. That such deprivations do not occur suddenly, but we become habituated and inured to them, does not alter their significance.

It is also important to remember that the causes of global poverty may not be very different from the causes of poverty within Britain. The distribution of power and the marginalisation of the poor; the ownership of capital and access to land or housing; unequal growth of different regions and the migration of the skilled away from poorer regions; differences in access to education – whether primary schools or universities – and to health – whether clean water or a healthy diet; the power of multinationals – whether controlling production or consumption patterns: all these are common to richer and poorer countries. There is much to be learned by seeing ourselves as others see us. For example, the British Government's new concern with poverty in Africa may be welcome but it largely ignores the ways in which Britain in the past devastated and even now continues to impoverish the continent. In myriad ways, from the finance of the monarchy to the subsidy of arms exports, Britain continues to finance privilege and power relations that perpetuate poverty.

What do we mean by child poverty?

Much effort has been devoted to defining what is child poverty and what is the appropriate poverty line. This is not the place to set out or scrutinise different approaches (a summary is provided in Flaherty et al).[5] Some conclusions are widely accepted:

1. **Poverty** should be defined as a situation where resources are less than needs or below a defined poverty line.
   Needs must be defined relative to prevailing living standards in society. This is true both conceptually and empirically. Conceptually, as Townsend put it:

   > Individuals, families and groups in the population can be said to be in poverty when they lack the resources to obtain the types of diet, participate in the activities and have the living conditions and amenities which are customary, or at least widely encouraged or approved, in societies to which they belong.[6]

   Empirical studies of what people regard as an appropriate poverty line, or the minimum necessary to live on, show that this has increased as average living standards have improved.

2. The **poverty line** must take account of the size of the household. There are differences over which 'equivalence' scale is best but results using the McClements scale or the Organisation for Economic Co-operation and Development scale are not overall very different.[7]

3. There are many possible measures of **resources** – whether income, assets, public services, capabilities or other measures – of the unit to

be considered – whether the household, the family or the individual – and the relevant time period – whether over a week, a year, even a lifetime. In practice, the most accessible and relevant measure for which data can be compared over a number of years is equivalised household weekly income after tax and benefits. Because of variations in housing costs and benefits, which bear little relation to differences in housing quality, where possible the measure used here is based on income after housing costs.[8]

4. **Child poverty** – inadequacy of resources children enjoy relative to their needs – is not directly measurable. The nearest proxy is to assess the resources of the family in which the child lives relative to the poverty line. (Children living in institutions are omitted from most poverty statistics – see Chapter 12 on care leavers.) It must be recognised that children in some non-poor families are deprived of an adequate share of resources and so are poor; similarly, in many poor families the mother makes personal sacrifices to prevent the child(ren) being in poverty. It must also be recognised that in some cases resources are used in ways that do not best meet the needs of the children – but this is a matter of judgement that only obfuscates discussions of child, or family, poverty.

What, then, is the poverty line most commonly used in Britain? It is 60 per cent of median income after housing costs. For 2003/04 this was:[9]

- Single parent, one child aged 5   £135 a week
- Couple, one child aged 8   £219 a week
- Couple, two children aged 5 and 11   £262 a week
- Couple, three children aged 5, 8 and 11   £303 a week

The Government report on *Measuring Child Poverty*[10] recommended three components for a combined long-term measure of child poverty:

- an 'absolute low income' measure of whether the poorest families are seeing their incomes rise in real terms;
- a 'relative low income' measure of whether the poorest families are keeping pace with the growth of incomes in the economy as a whole; *and*
- a measure combining 'material deprivation and relative low income' to provide a wider measure of people's living standards.

The report concludes: 'Using this measure, poverty is falling when all three indicators are moving in the right direction'.[11] The relative measure will almost certainly be the hardest to achieve. Relative measures are used throughout this chapter.

Child poverty in Britain

Poverty among children in Britain is more common than among adults of working age and, more surprisingly, more common than among pensioners. The extent of child poverty in Britain using the latest available data is shown in Table 1.1 overleaf. It is clear that the extent of child poverty varies greatly by family type, by economic status, by housing tenure, by ethnic group and, to a lesser extent, by region. The proportion of children in poverty in two-parent families ranged from 3 per cent where both parents were in full-time work to 77 per cent where neither parent was in paid work. Children in lone-parent families were more than twice as likely to be in poverty as those in two-parent families. Over half in tenant households were poor compared to 15 per cent in owner-occupied housing. Children in Pakistani/Bangladeshi families were by far the most likely to be in poverty. Despite their proximity, the lowest regional rate was in South East England and the highest in Inner London.

Why was child poverty so high? The Treasury's *Child Poverty Review* offered an explanation of child poverty:

> The UK has had one of the worst records on child poverty among industrialised nations. The proportion of children living in households with below 60 per cent of contemporary median income more than doubled between the later 1970s and mid 1990s. This was largely due to: demographic changes, in particular a growth in the number of lone parent families; a concentration of worklessness among low-skilled households; and a widening wage distribution with increased in-work poverty and weaker work incentives.
>
> Within households, child poverty can also be associated with a change in family circumstances, such as losing a job, having a baby, relationship breakdown or bereavement. Families who face barriers to the financial and other support and services they need to cope with these transitions can fall into poverty. If the family experiences several such events, the risks to children can increase.[12]

Table 1.1

Child poverty, 2003-04

	Proportion of children in poor families	Number of children in poor families
All children	28%	3.5m
Family type		
Children in:		
Lone-parent family	48%	1.5m
Two-parent family	21%	2.0m
Children in family with:		
1 child	24%	0.7m
2 children	24%	1.3m
3 children	29%	0.8m
4 or more children	51%	0.7m
Age of mother		
Under 25	52%	0.3m
25–34	35%	1.3m
35–44	23%	1.5m
45 and over	21%	0.4m
Age of youngest child		
Under 5	30%	1.5m
5–10	29%	1.3m
10–15	24%	0.6m
16–18	16%	0.1m
Economic status		
Children in:		
Lone-parent family		
In full-time work	9%	0.05m
In part-time work	27%	0.2m
Not in paid work	74%	1.2m
Two-parent family		
Both in full-time work	3%	0.05m
One in full-time, one in part-time work	6%	0.2m
One in full-time work, one not working	21%	0.5m
Both not in paid work	77%	0.6m
Other (self-employed and only part-time work)	36%	0.7m
Tenure		
Tenant	56%	2.2m
Owner-occupier	15%	1.3m

Ethnic group

White	25%	2.8m
Mixed	44%	0.05m
Indian	42%	0.1m
Pakistani/Bangladeshi	63%	0.3m
Black and Black British	49%	0.2m
Chinese or other ethnic group	52%	0.1m

Region

North East	30%	0.2m
North West and Merseyside	29%	0.4m
Yorkshire and Humberside	29%	0.3m
East Midlands	25%	0.2m
West Midlands	32%	0.4m
Eastern	22%	0.3m
Inner London	51%	0.3m
Outer London	34%	0.3m
South East	19%	0.3m
South West	26%	0.3m
Scotland	25%	0.3m
Wales	27%	0.2m

Source: National Statistics, *Households Below Average Income, 1994/5–2003/04*, Department for Work and Pensions, 2005, Tables E3.1, E4.1, 4.7 (AHC), 4.8 (AHC), 4.9 (AHC)

The Treasury's *Child Poverty Review* also summarised the effects:

> Child poverty:
> - damages childhood experience through limiting access to activities, services and opportunities, increasing exposure to risks, and diminishing access to the resources and support that increase resilience. All these can lead to bad outcomes for poor children;
> - contributes to and can result from social exclusion, a shorthand term for what can happen when people or areas suffer from linked problems such as unemployment, poor skills, poor housing, high crime, bad health and family breakdown;
> - denies equality of opportunity which can eventually blight adult life, leading to cycles of disadvantage.

While some children who grow up in low-income households will go on to achieve their full potential, many others will not. Poverty places strains on family life and excludes children from the everyday activities of their peers.

Many children experiencing poverty have limited opportunities to play safely and often live in overcrowded and inadequate housing, eat less nutritious food, suffer more accidents and ill health and have more problems with school work.

Much evidence exists of the link between growing up in a low-income household and experiencing a specific outcome, such as low educational attainment. Some children not only live in low-income families, but experience other poor outcomes, sometimes in combination with one another, reinforcing the need for a broad anti-poverty strategy that looks across the range of public services and welfare reform.[13]

Changes in child poverty

The changing proportion of children in poverty since 1979 is shown in Figure 1.1. The most striking fact is that the risk of a child being in poverty more than doubled between 1979 and the 1990s and, despite some reduction since 1998/99, is still twice as prevalent as is 1979.

The changes and prospects since 1997 are discussed further on pp14–16. In this section we consider why child poverty grew so appallingly

Figure 1.1

Child poverty 1979–2003/04

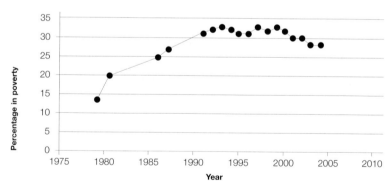

Source: National Statistics, *Households Below Average Income, 1994/5–2003/04*, Department for Work and Pensions, 2005, Table H6

between 1979 and 1996/97. The changing situation of children and rates of poverty are shown in Table 1.2.

Table 1.2
Child poverty, 1979 and 1996/97

	Situation of children		Proportion in poverty	
	1979	1996/97	1979	1996/97
	(%)	(%)	(%)	(%)
No full-time worker				
Lone parent	7	19	28	73
Couple with children	11	13	45	73
One or more full-time worker				
Employee, 1 or 2 children	50	39	1	8
Employee, 3+ children	23	15	5	24
Self-employed	9	13	19	28
All	**100**	**100**	**10**	**35**

Source: National Statistics, *Households Below Average Income 1979–1996/7*, Department of Social Security, 1998, Tables B3, F3 (AHC)

Part of the growth in poverty was due to the increased extent of unemployed and lone-parent families, which have always been more prone to poverty. Most of the change (85 per cent of it[14]) was due to the increased extent of poverty in each type of household. This resulted from greater inequality in earnings, the failure of most benefits to keep up with earnings, and tax changes that hurt the poor.

How and why does child poverty differ between countries?

The rate of child poverty in the 15 European Union (EU) countries is shown in Table 1.3 overleaf. In 2001 the UK rate was fifth highest – substantially higher than in Belgium, France, Germany and the Netherlands and over three times the rate of Denmark, Finland and Sweden. Why the UK has, as a proportion, so much more child poverty than the last group must be a cause for concern. The difference strongly suggests there is nothing inevitable about such a high rate of child poverty.

If rates of child poverty for different family types are compared, as is also shown in Table 1.3, it is clear that the biggest difference exists for lone parent families. Half of UK lone-parent families are in poverty, the highest rate in the EU and four times the rate of the Scandinavian countries.

Factors affecting child poverty are summarised in Table 1.4. The UK had a substantially higher proportion of lone-parent families in the population than other EU countries. This, combined with the high rate of poverty among these families, accounts for a substantial part of the UK's high child poverty rate. Second, there is in Britain an exceptionally high proportion of children in jobless households – which is only partially explained by the joblessness in lone-parent families. Third, relatively low pay is common in families with children in the UK and the extent of low pay is

Table 1.3

Rates of poverty, EU 2001

Country	Children 0–15 years[a]	Single adults with children[b]	2 adults 1 child[b]	2 adults 2 children[b]	2 adults 3+ children[b]
UK	24	50	8	12	30
Austria	13	23	7	7	23
Belgium	12	25	7	11	7
Denmark	7	12	3	3	13
Finland	6	11	5	5	5
France	18	35	10	12	24
Germany	14	36	9	7	21
Greece	18	37	8	14	26
Ireland	26	42	17	17	37
Italy	25	23	13	21	37
Luxembourg	18	35	13	15	23
Netherlands	16	45	10	9	17
Portugal	27	39	9	15	49
Spain	26	42	18	23	34
Sweden	7	13	5	4	8

Sources:

a. European Commission, *Draft Joint Inclusion Report: statistical annex*, COM (2003) 773 final, Commission of the European Communities, 2003, Table 1

b. Ibid., Table 9

indicated by the comparatively low level of the minimum wage, being only 30 per cent of mean earnings in the UK compared to over one-half in some EU countries. More positively, in effect picking up some of the pieces, social transfers ranked fifth in the EU so that redistribution through the social security system prevents there being even more child poverty.

Table 1.4

Factors affecting child poverty

Country	Proportion of population in lone parent families 2002[a]	Children in jobless households[b]	Minimum wage as proportion of mean earnings[c]	Effect of social transfers[d]
	(%)	(%)	(%)	(%)
UK	8	17	30	16
Austria	3	4	–	22
Belgium	4	14	52	14
Denmark	6	–	57	20
Finland	3	–	–	12
France	2	9	51	14
Germany	6	9	–	6
Greece	4	5	42	6
Ireland	5	11	46	10
Italy	5	7	51	5
Luxembourg	2	3	44	20
Netherlands	2	7	44	12
Portugal	4	5	44	12
Spain	2	6	28	7
Sweden	3	–	–	15

Sources:

a. European Commission, *Draft Joint Inclusion Report: statistical annex*, COM (2003) 773 final, Commission of the European Communities, 2003, Table 1 Context Information

b. Ibid., Table 17

c. J Bradshaw and N Finch, *A Comparison of Child Benefit Packages in 22 Countries*, DWP Research Report No.174, Corporate Document Services, 2002, Table 2.7

d. Derived from European Commission, *Draft Joint Inclusion Report: statistical annex*, COM (2003) 773 final, Commission of the European Communities, 2003, Table 12

Developments since 1997[15]

The period since 1997 – effectively since 1999 – has seen more rapid government action against child poverty than at any previous time. New benefits and tax credits have been introduced, existing benefits have been increased and many other measures have been taken to tackle poverty. The only exceptions to this trend were the abolition of one-parent benefit and the lone-parent premium in income support. The benefit and tax credit changes are summarised in Table 1.5; for comparison over the same period, average earnings of full-time employees rose in real terms by 12.1 per cent. Overall, government expenditure on child-contingent support rose by nearly 70 per cent in real terms between 1997/98 and 2002/03.

At the same time, unemployment fell, the national minimum wage was introduced and spending on childcare increased. All these changes resulted in a fall of 700,000 in the number of children in poverty between 1996/97 and 2003/04. Whether the target of reducing child poverty by one-quarter by 2004/05 will be met remains in doubt. It will at best be a close-run thing. What has, however, been clearly demonstrated is that

Table 1.5

Increases in child benefit, income support and net income after housing costs, 1997–2003 (£ a week, April 2003 prices)

	April 1997	April 2003	Change 1997–2003
	(£)	**(£)**	**(%)**
Child benefit (first child)	12.81	16.05	25.3
Child benefit (subsequent child)	10.43	10.75	3.1
Income support (lone parent, 1 child under 11)	91.18	108.90	19.4
Income support (couple, 1 child under 11)	116.87	140.00	19.8
Income support (couple, 2 children 11)	135.71	178.50	31.5
Net income after housing costs			
Couple, 2 children, on average earnings	311.73	352.00	12.9
Lone parent, 1 child, on average earnings	229.33	266.22	16.1
Couple, 2 children, on half average earnings	177.61	239.90	35.1
Lone parent, 1 child, on half average earnings	156.95	193.55	23.3

Source: K Stewart, 'Towards an equal start? Addressing childhood poverty and deprivation', Table 7.2, in J Hills and K Stewart (eds), *A More Equal Society?*, Policy Press, 2005

child poverty is not inevitable or inexorable. It can be and has been reduced – and tribute is due to the determination of the Chancellor of the Exchequer.

The reduction in child poverty has had a real impact on what cannot be afforded by lone parents, and on their financial stress, as shown in Table 1.6.

Table 1.6
Circumstances of lone parents: 1999 and 2002

	1999 (%)	2002 (%)
Unable to afford:		
Cooked main meal every day	8	3
Fresh fruit on most days	17	9
New, not second-hand, clothes when needed	41	25
One-week holiday away from home	74	58
Problems with debts almost all the time	15	12
Always runs out of money before end of week	27	19
Worries about money almost always	45	30
Never has money left over	48	17

Source: S McKay and S Collard, *Developing Deprivation Questions for the Family Resources Survey*, University of Bristol, 2003, Table 7.1

More sobering, the level of child poverty in 2004/05 remains twice what it was in 1979. There is a very long way to go to get back to the 1979 level, let alone abolish child poverty. The Government's next target is the halving of child poverty by 2010. For the House of Commons' report on child poverty, Holly Sutherland estimated the cost of reaching this target, an estimate endorsed by the Committee:

> To help reach the goal of halving child poverty by 2010, the Committee recommends that support for each of the poorest children measured on the after housing costs basis – soon be increased by £10 per week.[16]

The Committee also concluded:

> However, the Government's programme will not by itself deliver the child poverty reductions necessary to reach the 2010 goal merely by doing more of the same. A clear focus is now necessary on those areas and those

groups which present the greatest challenges to the achievement of the target.[17]

Part of the purpose of this book is to clarify some of 'the greatest challenges'.

Lessons for the future

There is a very long way to go to achieve the declared goal of abolishing child poverty in a generation. But some progress towards this goal has been made. This progress has benefited children in all family types, in all regions and in all neighbourhoods.[18]

The Government has defined its goals as 'work for those who can, security for those who cannot'. How far has it achieved these goals? The employment record since 1997 has generally been very good. Unemployment on the claimant count has fallen steadily from 1.6 million in 1997 to half that level in early 2005. It is true that among those aged 55 and over there has been a large increase in economic inactivity, with many more receiving sickness and invalidity benefits, but this age group has few dependent children so this change has had little impact on child poverty. There are two aspects of employment that are particularly relevant for child poverty.

First, employment of lone-parent families remains low. Between 1996/97 and 2002/03 the number of children in lone-parent families rose slightly from 2.9 million to 3.1 million; over this period the number whose parent was working full time rose from 0.4 million to 0.6 million. The Government's Public Service Agreement target is that 70 per cent of lone parents should be in employment by 2010, compared to the baseline of 53.4 per cent in 2003. But progress towards this has been slow, rising only by 7 per cent between 1997 and 2003. In part, this reflects the preference of many lone mothers to be at home with their children. In part, it is indicative of the complexity and cost of childcare and transport as well as problems finding suitable employment. The availability of advice through the New Deal for Lone Parents and the enhanced return to employment resulting from the minimum wage and the working and child tax credits both encourage entering and staying in paid employment. The failure of more to do so even when employment generally is buoyant shows how much needs to change if work (by which the Government means paid work) is to approach the target level, let alone match Scandinavian levels.

Second, it is becoming increasingly clear that work for many families with children is insecure and poorly rewarded. As McKnight[19] and Horgan[20] have shown, many of those on the margins of employment end up with incomes close to or below the poverty level. It is simply not the case, given the distribution of skills and earnings, that paid work is enough to prevent poverty. The notion that a wage is almost always a living wage sufficient to support a family is less true now than in the past. One remedy is for the Government to increase the tax credit subsidy to low earnings, though increased means testing has its own problems and dangers. Another remedy is to raise the national minimum wage, although this too has its limits. In the longer run, the goal must be to narrow the distribution of skills and earnings – in effect, to address broader issues of inequality rather than solely concentrating on poverty.

The complement to 'work for those who can' is 'security for those who cannot'. As has been seen, additions for children within social security have increased markedly faster than those for single people and childless couples. Yet, comparing the income support rates in Table 1.5 with the poverty lines shown at the start of this chapter (see p6), it is clear that the 'safety net' provided by the State is still far below its own poverty level. Indeed, the relative levels of the safety net for most families remain lower in 2004/05 than in 1994/95. All that can be said about this fact is that this situation is inconsistent, indefensible and shameful.

Child poverty is related to inequality more generally and to the state of the economy. As this book demonstrates, not all have benefited equally from growth but, in general, prosperity has reduced poverty not merely in absolute terms but also relatively. Recession brings rising unemployment and worsened employment opportunities for those such as lone parents on the margins of employment; it tends to add to poverty. It may not be true that a 'rising tide lifts all boats equally', but a falling tide leaves the most vulnerable boats scraping the bottom. To change the metaphor, growth may not 'trickle down' equally to all in society but lack of growth tends to hit the poorest most harshly.

The challenge ahead was set out by Sutherland et al.:[21]

> In 1999 a goal was set of halving child poverty by 2010 and a relative definition of poverty was clearly adopted. Even if this goal is achieved, relative poverty will still be higher than in 1979. It will be possible to stay on track to achieve this goal but to do so will require substantially more redistribution to

the poorest and continuing priority to be given to the goal of ending child poverty. Further reductions in child poverty are likely to be increasingly hard to achieve. Beyond child poverty, the task of ending poverty more generally remains to be tackled. Britain at the beginning of the twenty-first century remains a nation scarred by poverty.

There is nothing inevitable about child poverty. Perhaps the most important lesson of the past five years is that it can be reduced. To achieve this had a cost, but it is a cost that caused little complaint. That cost must also be compared with the far greater cost – in terms of childhoods diminished and lifetime prospects jeopardised – of failing to tackle child poverty. For each child brought up in poverty there is no second chance.

Notes

1 UNICEF, *Children Under Threat, The State of the World's Children 2005*, UNICEF, 2004
2 Disposable household income (equivalised), National Statistics, *Households Below Average Income, 1994/5–2002/03*, Department for Work and Pensions, 2005
3 Life expectancy of males at birth, 2001–03, London, National Statistics, 2004
4 Proportion not getting 5+ GCSEs at A*–C, ONS, *Focus on Social Inequalities*, National Statistics, 2004
5 J Flaherty, J Veit-Wilson and P Dornan, *Poverty: the facts*, 5th edition, CPAG, 2004
6 P Townsend, *Poverty in the United Kingdom*, Penguin, 1979, p31
7 Equivalisation is discussed in further detail in CPAG's briefing paper, *Key Findings from the 2003/04 Households Below Average Income Series*, 2005, which can be downloaded from www.cpag.org.uk
8 For details see National Statistics, *Households Below Average Income, 1994/5–2002/03*, Department for Work and Pensions, 2005
9 Based on Table C and Appendix 2 Table 2.1 (AHC), National Statistics, *Households Below Average Income, 1994/5–2003/04,* Department for Work and Pensions, 2005
10 DWP, *Measuring Child Poverty*, Department for Work and Pensions, 2003
11 Ibid., p1
12 HM Treasury, *Child Poverty Review*, The Stationery Office, 2004, pp15–16
13 Ibid., p15
14 Based on the methodology set out in Appendix 2 of H Sutherland, T Sefton, D Piachaud, *Poverty in Britain: the impact of government policy since 1997*, Joseph Rowntree Foundation, 2003

15 This section draws extensively on K Stewart, 'Towards an equal start? Addressing childhood poverty and deprivation', in J Hills and K Stewart (eds), *A More Equal Society?*, Policy Press, 2005

16 House of Commons Work and Pensions Committee, *Child Poverty in the UK*, The Stationery Office, 2004, para 235

17 Ibid., para 301

18 As shown by M Evans, M Noble, G Wright, G Smith, M Lloyd and C Dibben, *Growing Together, Growing Apart*, The Policy Press/Joseph Rowntree Foundation, 2002

19 A McKnight, 'From childhood poverty to labour market disadvantage', in J Bynner, P Elias, A McKnight, H Pan and G Pierre (eds), *Young People's Changing Routes to Independence*, York Publishing Services, 2002

20 G Horgan, 'Welfare-to-Work Policies and Child Poverty in Northern Ireland', *Social Policy and Administration*, 39:1, 2005

21 H Sutherland, T Sefton, D Piachaud, *Poverty in Britain: the impact of government policy since 1997*, Joseph Rowntree Foundation, 2003, p63

Two

The adequacy of benefits for children

Sue Middleton

Introduction

There are some doubts about whether the Government will meet the first of its targets for reducing child poverty – by one-quarter by 2004[1] – and concern that it will be even more difficult to achieve subsequent targets of reducing child poverty by half by 2010 and abolishing it by 2020. There can also be no doubt that the present Government has increased significantly the proportion of the nation's resources that are devoted to children. Adam and Brewer[2] estimate that government spending on 'child-contingent support' increased from £10 billion in 1975 to £22 billion in 2003; from 3.4 per cent to 4.7 per cent of total government spending. The effect of these increases can be seen in the sums that are available to parents bringing up children in the UK. Between 1997 and April 2004 child benefit increased by 49 per cent for the first child, from £11.05 to £16.50 a week, and by 23 per cent for a second child, from £9.00 to £11.05. Largely because of the introduction of the means-tested child tax credit, the oldest child in a family is now eligible for allowances of up to £47.72 a week each, compared with just £16.90 in 1997 for a child under the age of 11 years.

But are these current benefit levels adequate to keep children out of poverty? Equally, what does reducing the proportion of children living below 60 per cent of median income mean for children's lives? Is the standard of living that a family living on 60 per cent of median income experiences 'adequate' to keep children out of poverty? Answers to these questions are necessary if we are to be sure that meeting government targets on child poverty, as measured using the Government's preferred measures of relative income, absolute income, and material deprivation,[3] mean a genuine improvement in the lives of children that could indeed be said to represent an end to child poverty.

We also need a more accessible means of explaining what is meant by a 'low income' than the complex and obscure 60 per cent of median equivalised household income. Most people have no conception of what this means in monetary terms, or in terms of the standard of living that this allows people to achieve. This makes it difficult to get across the message that child poverty exists in the UK and needs to be addressed, as well as what poverty actually means in terms of children's lifestyles and living standards.

This chapter focuses on 'adequacy' or 'minimum income' standards and how these might be derived for children and used to assess the adequacy of benefits for children. The establishment of adequacy standards would not and should not replace the Government's preferred measures of childhood poverty. The 60 per cent of median income target must remain as the main means of monitoring government progress. But adequacy standards would provide a more transparent and accessible means of understanding what living on a low income means for children's lives, and be a useful benchmark for a range of provisions for children and families in addition to benefits, including child support arrangements and foster care allowances.

To date, the Government has set its face against the use of such standards to measure poverty. In a letter to Lord Morris of Manchester dated 8 March 2004, Tony Blair said, 'The Government does not think it is necessary to estimate a minimum income standard. Poverty is multi faceted and can only be gauged by indicators'. Malcolm Wicks (Minister of State, Work and Pensions Department, until May 2005) has referred to proposals for minimum income standards as 'the search for the Holy Grail', suggesting that it would be impossible to arrive at agreement about what should be included in such standards and, hence, what their level should be.

While there is no space in this chapter to debate at length the concept, definition and measurement of 'adequacy' as it might relate to children,[4] the central thrust is that it would be possible to arrive at a consensus about an adequacy standard for children, at least in monetary terms. The starting point is the seminal work of John Veit-Wilson, who emphasised that minimum income standards need to be monitored and that 'Good monitoring methods "triangulate" approaches to see how far different methods arrive at similar answers'.[5] This chapter seeks to take forward this suggestion of triangulation by using existing data from a range of sources to begin to assess the adequacy of current benefits for children. Data have been drawn from budget standards, expenditure and income-based measures of children's needs.

Budget standards

Budget standards involve the construction and costing of a basket of goods and services sufficient for a particular family to reach a predetermined standard of living. The budget standards can then be used for a number of purposes, of which measuring poverty and benefits adequacy is just one. A range of methods can be used to develop budget standards, mainly varying according to the selection of the predetermined standard of living, who makes the decisions about what should be included in the basket, and how these decisions are made. Traditionally, budget standards are constructed by committees of experts in, for example, nutrition, who decide what are the necessary components of a healthy diet in constructing the 'food basket'.

Budget standards drawn up using two methodologies are used in this chapter:

- **Family Budget Unit's (FBU's) Low Cost but Acceptable Budget.** This was originally developed in York in the early 1990s and extensively updated in 1998.[6] The Low Cost but Acceptable Budget shows 'how much it costs families in different circumstances to maintain indefinitely a living standard which, though simple, provides a healthy diet, material security, social participation and a sense of control – indefinitely'.[7] Initial budgets are drawn up by experts and are supplemented by data drawn from sources such as the *Family Expenditure Survey* (now the *Expenditure and Food Survey*). Budgets are discussed with focus groups of low-income families. Data in this chapter are taken from the Low Cost but Acceptable Budgets for Families with Children updated to April 2004 prices, which can be found on the FBU's website (www.york.ac.uk/res/fbu), and from separate tables showing the cost of children derived from the FBU's budgets.

- **Centre for Research in Social Policy's (CRSP's) Consensual Budget Standards (CBS)**. This method for deriving budget standards asks ordinary people living in the circumstances for which a budget standard is to be constructed to act as their own budget standards committees.[8] For children, for example, socio-economically mixed focus groups of parents decide what should be included in the basket of goods and services to allow children to live a 'minimum essential' lifestyle. This is defined according to the UN Convention on the Rights of the Child as 'the right of every child to a standard of living adequate for the child's physical, mental, spiritual, moral and social development'.[9] Two CBS are used in this chapter: a CBS for children in the UK originally developed in 1994[10] and a CBS for Jersey developed between 1998 and 2002.[11]

It should be noted that each of these budget standards has difficulties that need to be borne in mind in what follows. First, both the original FBU and the CRSP CBS for children in the UK are over 10 years old and are in need of re-basing. While updating for changes in the retail price index (RPI) provides an indication of the additional cost of providing the original baskets of goods and services, patterns of consumption may well have changed over the intervening period, and needs may be perceived to have changed as a result. Secondly, the CBS for Jersey were drawn up according to the priorities of people living in Jersey, which are not necessarily the same for people living in the UK. The cost of living is very much higher in Jersey and, while the Jersey CBS have been reduced by 45 per cent to allow for these differences,[12] the baskets of goods and services on which they are based might be slightly different for the UK. Thirdly, both methods set out to establish living standards which, while acceptable, are very low. Whether the resulting living standards are 'adequate' for children in Britain at the start of the 21st century needs further debate.

Expenditure data

For this analysis data have been drawn from the *Small Fortunes* survey of the lifestyles and living standards of British children.[13] This provides nationally representative figures of what families spent on individual children in 1994, and is still the only source of such data. Again, it will be noted that these data are old and have been uprated to 2004 prices using the RPI.

Income

Finally, income data are used to give an indication of what 60 per cent of median income represents in money terms.[14] Specifically, the figures are taken from Table 2.3 in the latest *Households Below Average Income* report, which takes levels of equivalised income for the population as a whole and translates them into cash equivalents for different family types. The figures used are after housing costs and include self-employed people.

Benefits

For the purposes of this chapter we have chosen to focus on the maximum benefits to which children and their families would be entitled if on income support (or non-contributory jobseeker's allowance) and receiving the maximum amount of child tax credit. In other words, it has been assumed that no adult in the child's family is working. It is, of course, possible to calculate benefit adequacy for a range of scenarios where adults are working at different wage rates and for varying hours. However, it was decided to focus on income support for a number of reasons:

- Income support rates for adults remain low, hence undermine the growth in incomes as a result of increases in child tax credit. Compared to the significant increases in benefits for children described earlier in this chapter, income support rates for adults have increased by relatively small amounts; for example, the rate for couples over the age of 18 has increased by only 13 per cent since 1997, from £77.15 a week to £87.30 a week.

- Children in families on income support have a very high risk of poverty according to the Government's own figures; 74 per cent of such children (2 million children) lived in families with incomes below 60 per cent of the median after housing costs in 2003/04.[15] It is particularly valuable, therefore, to see what adequacy standards can tell us about the levels of benefit that might be needed to take children out of poverty.

- The statement which people receive informing them of the amount of income support to which they are entitled says that this is the amount that the law says they need to live on each week. Therefore, it is particularly illuminating to compare the amounts suggested by 'adequacy standards' with the amount which the law says is adequate. Data on benefit levels have been taken from the Department for Work and Pensions and the Revenue websites.

In what follows the comparisons should be regarded as indicative, rather than conclusive. The aim is to show how data from different sources might be triangulated to assess the adequacy of benefits, rather than to reach firm conclusions.

Benefit adequacy in 2004

The first part of this analysis focuses on the adequacy of benefits for the whole family, using two families as examples – a couple and a lone mother, each with a boy aged 10 and a girl aged 4. The second piece of analysis focuses on measures for the same two children as individuals.

Families

Figure 2.1 overleaf compares income support rates for couple and lone-parent families with CBS Jersey and FBU budget standards and with 60 per cent of median income, as follows:

- FBU = Family Budget Unit's budget standards for a couple and a lone mother, each with a boy aged 10 and a girl aged 4, and no earners. The figures include a small amount for alcohol and for a car in order to be comparable with the CRSP Jersey budgets. The figures were uprated by the FBU to April 2004 prices.

- CBS Jersey = CRSP's Consensual Budget Standards for households in Jersey 2001, uprated to June 2004 using the Jersey RPI, then reduced by 45 per cent to reflect the higher costs of living in Jersey. Budgets are for a couple with children and a single adult, each with a first child aged 10 and a second child aged 4 of a different gender.

- Benefits = income support payments, child benefit and child tax credits at April 2004. Includes family premium, excludes housing benefit and council tax benefit.

- Income = 60 per cent weekly median income after housing costs for a couple with two children aged 5 and 11.

Figure 2.1

Adequacy of benefits for families on income support

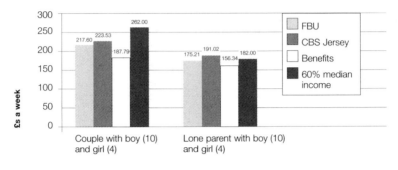

The first point to note about Figure 2.1 is the similarity between the FBU and CBS budget standards for children in both couple and lone-parent families. In both cases the CBS budgets are slightly higher than the FBU budgets – by 2.7 per cent for couple families and by 9 per cent for lone-parent families. It seems that using quite different budget standard methodologies has led to very similar conclusions about how an adequate income might look. Second, benefits remain significantly below the levels of adequacy suggested by the budget standards. A couple family on income support would need a benefit increase of 16 per cent to achieve the FBU standard of living, and 19 per cent to meet the CBS Jersey budget standard. The gaps for lone-parent families are 12 per cent (FBU) and 22 per cent (CBS Jersey). Third, 60 per cent of median income is very much higher than either benefits or the budget standards for the couple family. The couple family would need an extra £74.21 each week, or an increase in benefits of 40 per cent to move the family to 60 per cent of median income.

Children

Figure 2.2 opposite looks in more detail at the circumstances of the two children in our model families. The FBU budgets, which are prepared for 'model' families, do not easily allow the costs of children to be extracted. This analysis, therefore, focuses on two CBS measures.

- CBS UK = minimum essential budgets for a pre-school and primary school aged child, childcare excluded.

- CBS Jersey = minimum essential budgets for a pre-school and primary school aged child, childcare excluded.

- Benefits = maximum amount of child tax credit and child benefit for a boy aged 10 and a girl aged 4 living in the same family (£47.72 for the older child and £42.27 for the younger). The family addition in income support has been excluded.

- Average spending = *Small Fortunes* weekly regular spending on pre-school and primary school aged children.

- As in the previous analysis, all figures are for prices or benefits in April 2004.

The CBS UK, which is the oldest budget standard, produces the lowest figures for both children, emphasising the need for these budgets to be re-based. The CBS Jersey is highest for the 4-year-old girl, while the average spending figure is highest for the 10-year-old boy. All three measures are above the current maximum rate of benefits for the 4-year-old girl, which would need to be increased by between 14 per cent and 46 per cent according to the measure chosen. For the 10-year-old boy, benefits

Figure 2.2
Adequacy of benefits for children

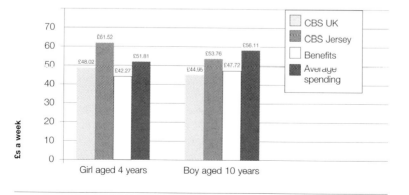

are higher than the CBS UK by 6 per cent but are lower than either the average spending or CBS Jersey figures by 22 per cent and 13 per cent respectively.

Conclusion

In general, benefit levels for families and for children remain inadequate to purchase even the restricted standard of living implied by the budget standards and expenditure data used in this analysis. But can we reach a conclusion about what would be an adequate benefit level for children on the basis of these figures? The answer is, not at the moment. It can be argued that neither the CBS nor FBU budgets provide for an 'adequate' standard of living in 2005. Both were set at a low level, to allow a Low Cost but Acceptable standard of living in the case of the former and a minimum essential standard of living in the FBU. It might be argued that these definitions of living standards are unacceptably low. Furthermore, both sets of budgets and the expenditure data included here are out of date and might, again, be underestimates of an adequate living standard for families and children in 2005.

In order to take this work forward a Minimum Living Standards Commission is urgently needed to oversee and co-ordinate the further work that is required. Social scientists need to update and expand budget standards, to exploit further other existing sources of data, and to explore variations in needs arising from cultural and geographical differences, or costs related to disability. Science needs to ensure that adequacy standards are sufficient for nutrition and healthy development.

It is not the role of government to set adequacy standards. As Veit-Wilson contends:

> ...the needs of beneficiaries for a level of living minimally adequate to meet the demands of human dignity and participation in a specified social context cannot be described or measured simply in terms of prescriptions by politicians, however benevolent.[16]

Government will always set benefit levels, which may or may not achieve adequacy standards, against other priorities for taxation and public expenditure. It is then for the electorate to judge whether the Government's priorities are correct.

Notes

1   See, for example, H Sutherland, T Sefton and D Piachaud, *Poverty in Britain: the impact of government policy since 1997*, Joseph Rowntree Foundation, 2003

2   S Adam and M Brewer, *The Financial Costs and Benefits of Supporting Children Since 1975*, Joseph Rowntree Foundation, 2004

3   DWP, *Measuring Child Poverty*, Department for Work and Pensions, 2003

4   See C Corrigan, *Exploring an Income Adequacy Standard for Children*, Combat Poverty Agency Working Paper 04/02 October, 2004; J Veit-Wilson, *Setting Adequacy Standards: how governments define minimum incomes*, Policy Press, 1998 for useful discussions of these issues

5   J Veit-Wilson, *Setting Adequacy Standards: how governments define minimum incomes*, Policy Press, 1998, p109

6   H Parker (ed.), *Low Cost but Acceptable: a minimum income standard for the UK: families with young children*, Policy Press, 1998

7   Ibid., p10

8   See S Middleton, *Budget Standards for Jersey: a handbook*, CRSP Working Paper 444, Centre for Research in Social Policy, 2002 for a detailed description of the CBS methodology

9   United Nations Convention on the Rights of the Child, Article 27

10 S Middleton, K Ashworth and R Walker, *Family Fortunes: pressures on parents and children in the 1990s*, CPAG, 1994

11 S Middleton, *Budget Standards for Jersey: a handbook*, CRSP Working Paper 444, Centre for Research in Social Policy, 2002

12 This figure is based on calculations undertaken by the Statistics Section of the States of Jersey, which compared expenditure in the *Jersey Household Expenditure Survey* with the *Expenditure and Food Survey*

13 S Middleton, K Ashworth and I Braithwaite, *Small Fortunes: spending on children, childhood poverty and parental sacrifice*, Joseph Rowntree Foundation, 1997

14 National Statistics, *Households Below Average Income, 1994/5–2003/04*, Department for Work and Pensions, 2005

15 Ibid., Table 4.8

16 J Veit-Wilson, *Setting Adequacy Standards: how governments define minimum incomes*, Policy Press, 1998, p110

Three

Working a way out of poverty?

Paul Dornan

Introduction

Work – more accurately, paid work – is fundamental to the strategy intended by the current Government to bring about the eradication of child poverty. In the 2004 *Child Poverty Review*,[1] work is articulated as 'the best form of welfare'.[2] Indeed, as Sue Middleton shows in Chapter 2, since assistance benefits are paid below the level of the poverty line, for most families work is the only route out of poverty. If paid work is to be central to the eradication of child poverty, two questions need answering in the context of this book:

- How much can work be made to address family poverty?
- Where do the gains from work-focused policy bite? Will they help children at the greatest risk of poverty?

Addressing the first question, this chapter argues that increasing labour market incomes has a considerable role to play, backed by other income protection measures, in reducing child poverty. In answering the second question, since many of the poorest children have parents who face the most difficult, sometimes intractable, barriers to paid work, they are inevitably the hardest to help in this way. Policy intended to increase the opportunities, the training and the support to facilitate paid work is welcome, but there is much further to go yet in truly overcoming barriers to work. Work-focused social policy also needs to recognise – in practice as well as rhetoric – that there are many children for whom parental work does not provide a route out of poverty; to eradicate child poverty these children need an adequate safety net.

Since 1997, the overall employment rate has increased[3] and government policy appears set to push it higher. In October 2004 Tony Blair suggested a substantial target of 1.5 million more adults in employment.[4] Increases in the employment rate and the introduction of tax credits have been associated with falls in the rate of child poverty. The period from spring 1997 to autumn 2004 has seen a reduction of 426,000 in the number of children living in workless households. However, there are still 1.7 million children living in workless households.[5]

Increased participation in the labour market has been driven by a growing and stable economy along with labour interventions, particularly the New Deals tailored around specific groups, aimed at increasing the employment rate where it was seen to be low. Intervention has been backed by Public Service Agreements (PSAs 1, 3, 4 and 8)[6] which specify not only the aim to address worklessness per se, but to target lone parents, ethnic minorities, those aged over 50, those with few qualifications, those living in specific local authorities with low employment rates, and disabled adults. Although working tax credit (WTC) has increased the wage rates for those in receipt, especially for families,[7] it has done so at the expense of a larger pool of low-paid workers who face high marginal deduction rates.[8]

The crossover between groups targeted by work-focused policy and the children detailed in the rest of this book is substantial. Many of the groups of children under discussion in this book have parents who face either very significant barriers which prevent or constrain labour market earnings or have earnings that are simply insufficient to meet need. Since the tendency of the market is to draw in those 'easiest' to employ first – and quite possibly also to eject those most 'difficult' to employ in recession – those likely to gain first, and most, from labour market growth are not likely to be the children discussed here. Policy – though focused on the greatest areas of worklessness – continues to face significant difficulty in overcoming these barriers. The extent to which the Government will be successful in its objectives, and the extent to which this will lead to good quality jobs – jobs which actually protect children from poverty – remains to be seen.

Parents have the primary responsibility for providing for their children,[9] but it is for the State to ensure parents are able to do so. If gains from work cannot protect children from poverty then, for both moral and practical reasons, responsibility for this should fall on society via benefits and tax credits.

The 1990 UN Convention on the Rights of the Child, signed by the UK Government, specified the need for a minimum standard of living in Article 27, clause one.

Clause two specifies that:

> The parent(s) or others responsible for the child have the primary responsi-
> bility to secure, within their abilities and financial capacities, the conditions of
> living necessary for the child's development.

Clause three outlines the responsibilities of the State:

> States Parties, in accordance with national conditions and within their
> means, shall take appropriate measures to assist parents and others
> responsible for the child to implement this right and shall in case of need
> provide material assistance and support programmes, particularly with
> regard to nutrition, clothing and housing.

The State has responsibility to ensure parents are able to work and therefore to remove barriers to employment. However, the emphasis placed on
paid work in protecting children from poverty must not obfuscate the need
for an adequate safety net to protect those children for whom parental
employment is either not an option or whose parents are engaged in low-
paid or part-time work which does not protect them adequately from
poverty.

Paid work and protecting children from poverty

The associations between employment and income poverty are made all
too obvious in the 2003/04 *Households Below Average Income* report.[10]
A couple of key statistics demonstrate the variation in child poverty risk
which is associated with work patterns of adult household members:

- No adult in paid work   77 per cent of children
  (couple and single combined)   are income poor

- Two full-time workers   3 per cent of children
                                   are income poor

The risk of a child being income poor is **25.7 times greater** if s/he lives
in a household with no adult in paid work compared with a child living in
a couple household where both parents work full time.

If in 2003/04 all children had the same risk of being income poor as children with two parents in full-time work (3 per cent), then there would have been 375,000 children living in poverty – one-tenth of the actual number counted as poor in the same year – and the Government would comfortably meet its ambition of a child poverty rate 'among the best in Europe'.[11]

Unfortunately, therein lies the flaw: not all children have two parents; not all parents can work; and even if parents can work, they cannot necessarily be assumed to be able to work full time. Each of these permutations is associated with an increased risk of a child being income poor over that of children growing up with two adults who are in full-time work. Again, some simple comparisons:[12]

Risk of child poverty (per cent)	Lone parent	Couple
All adults working full time	9	3
One adult working full time	9	21
One adult working full time, one part time	–	6
One or more in part-time work	27	55
No adult in work	74	77

The 'gold standard', in terms of the lowest risk of a child enduring income poverty, is for her/him to live with two parents, and for both of these to be in full-time work. This is the experience of only one in ten children.

To have only one parent, though still in full-time work, triples the risk. For couples, having one workless adult in the household is associated with an increased risk, largely the effect of the additional needs (adjusted for by the process of equivalisation) of having two adults plus children met by only one salary.

Full-time work, with a presumed higher income, offers much greater protection than part-time work. For lone parents, working part time rather than full time is associated with a three times greater risk of the child being income poor. The equivalent figure for couples is much greater (18.3 times).

The chances of a child being income poor if all adults in her/his household are not working, as discussed above, are truly terrible.

As Jane Millar and Karen Gardiner have recently written about adults in an analysis of low pay and poverty:

> ...more accurate than the slogan 'work is the best route out of poverty' is
> the following statement: having a job and living with other people with jobs
> is the most likely way of avoiding poverty.[13]

Making work deliver – what about children at the greatest risk of poverty?

Children at the greatest risk of poverty are very likely to have parents who
face either barriers to work or low labour market income. In addition – a
point returned to in the concluding section – the chapters in this book
illustrate the close relationship between childhood poverty and lower educational attainment, likely to lead to a weakened labour market position
and relatively low wages. This chapter considers disadvantages in terms
of worklessness, wage inequality and barriers to work.

Worklessness

'Worklessness' is not unemployment (though it does also cover this): it
refers to those without a job either because they do not have one, or they
are available for work and are looking (unemployment), or they are simply
unable to work, either due to incapacity or caring responsibilities. The
worklessness of parents is closely associated with a considerably
increased risk of a child being in poverty. Reducing worklessness, as an
objective, must therefore be sensitive not only to barriers to work but to
the personal circumstances of those currently workless.

Figure 3.1 opposite reproduces data from a key strategy document
(*Opportunity for All*) on groups currently targeted by policy, showing just
how variable the employment rates are. There are considerable gaps
between the overall employment rate and that experienced by the groups
indicated in the chart. Though there is some evidence of convergence
between the general trend and that for those aged over 50, the gap for
other groups remains very considerable. Employment rates have
increased – with the very significant and worrying exception of the falling
employment rate for those with low skills (defined in *Opportunity for All* as
the 15 per cent of working age adults with the lowest qualifications). This
chart does not, however, reveal how far the respective employment rates
of these groups can increase. It also contains more aggregate level data

Figure 3.1

Employment rates 1992–2004 (*Opportunity for All* indicators)

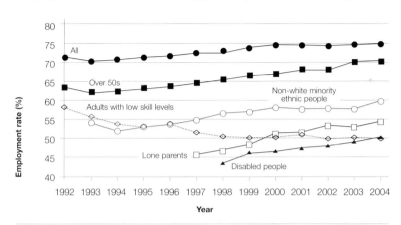

Source: Data taken from DWP, *Opportunity for All*, Sixth Annual Report, Cm 6239, Department for Work and Pensions, 2004, p180

than the later chapters of this book suggest – true variation within groups will be much greater.

Turning from the experience of *adults* to that of the 1.7 million *children* in the UK living in households where no parent worked in autumn 2004, *Labour Force Survey* figures[14] demonstrate not only the numbers but the respective risks by household type and, unsurprisingly, these closely link to the trends revealed in Figure 3.1. The chances of a child living in a workless household are much greater if s/he lives in a lone-parent household, affecting around half (47.6 per cent) of children of lone parents, compared to 5.5 per cent of children in couple households. Children living in lone-parent households make up much the largest proportion of all children in workless households (68.9 per cent). Nationally around 15.3 per cent of children lived in workless households, and most regions are broadly similar to this. The risk, however, for children in inner London (34.9 per cent) was over double the national average while the risk in the geographically proximate South East of England (9.4 per cent) was just two-thirds the average.

In terms of the proportion of children of a particular ethnicity living in a workless household, again the variation is considerable – from the lowest risk, 8 per cent of children of Indian origin and 13.3 per cent of white children, up to two-fifths (42.5 per cent) of children of Black African origin and one-third of Pakistani and Bangladeshi children (29.2 per cent). The picture is made more complex, and more compelling, by examining it in relation to working households (defined by National Statistics in terms of all available adults in work), demonstrating a variation from the highest proportion of children with all of the adults in their house in work of 57.6 per cent for white children, to just 10.5 per cent of Pakistani/ Bangladeshi children.

The scale of variations in worklessness is considerable and since paid work is required by most families to escape poverty, this brings with it significant problems of child poverty. There are, however, unsurprising associations between those least likely to be in employment and barriers to work. Anti-poverty policy needs to recognise this, not only in support-ing people to enter work but also in providing a more adequate safety net to underpin this strategy.

Wage inequality

The 2003/04 *Households Below Average Income* shows about half of all poor children live in households with one or more adult in paid work.[15] For children in working poor families, work does not offer a route out of pover-ty, resulting from a combination of low wages and fewer hours worked. The national minimum wage is a flagship policy but is currently set well below the level that a family would require to make ends meet without tax credits.[16] The in-work subsidy through WTC is important – particularly for families – though it both masks the level of market-generated low pay and it means that increased hours or pay are heavily taxed through lost WTC.[17]

Figure 3.2 opposite demonstrates the wage inequality generated by the market, separated out for men and women. This chart demonstrates not only high wage inequality, but the degree to which this is affected by gender. Women are much more likely than men to be concentrated in low-paid brackets, presumably as a result of both the gender-related pay gap and their increased likelihood of working part time. Working tax credit increases the earnings of the lowest paid, and so increases net pay and reduces some of the extremes demonstrated in the chart, though it is questionable whether such a substantial in-work means-tested subsidy is a sustainable solution to market inequality in the long term. Even after the intervention of WTC, inequality in incomes remains enormous, as is wit-nessed in very considerable net income inequality: in 2003/04 the poorest

Figure 3.2

Gross weekly earnings of employee respondents to the *New Earnings Survey* in 2003

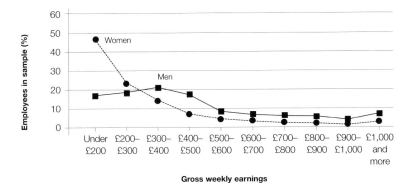

Source: Analysis of National Statistics, *Labour Market New Earnings Survey*, 2003, Table A32, figures for Great Britain. Reproduced from Child Poverty Action Group manifesto, *Ten Steps to a Society Free of Child Poverty*, CPAG, 2005.

fifth had a weekly income of £128, while the richest fifth had nearly five times as much at £616.[18]

Barriers to work

Barriers to work repeatedly occur as an issue in the chapters of this book. They significantly determine the family incomes of the groups described and the risk of children being in poverty. Barriers stem from the interrelationship between structural factors and those related to the personal circumstances of the adults concerned. Barriers impact upon employment, hours worked, pay received and progression. They constrain not only individual chances to take up employment but job opportunities themselves. Before briefly examining some of the barriers, underlying any analysis is a fundamental issue of 'work–life balance'. Increases in parental work effort mean less time spent caring for children. The long-term solution to child poverty should certainly involve greater labour market income for lower-income families, but this ought to be achieved through increased wage rates, not just longer hours.

Cutting across both in-work poverty and worklessness are the employment skills of parents, in so far as these determine access to good-quality, well-paid employment and progression within employment. David Piachaud (in Chapter 1) argues that the long-term solution to poverty is skills investment, focused on the poorest, to improve (and equalise) labour market incomes. The Government has demonstrated its interest in this area in a recent White Paper.[19] Improvements in skill levels across the population will take time, however, and the issue applies equally to adults and to children. As detailed in a number of chapters in this book, the current circumstances of children reduce their chances of gaining the qualifications that will assist them in the labour market. Access to good-quality education and training is clearly fundamental but – for the moment – child poverty is a barrier to this. Interventions to reduce child poverty should therefore also pay off in improved skills. Existing poverty and educational disadvantage – discussed in later chapters in this book – show the scale of the problems yet to be tackled.

Parental disability is associated with high levels of child income poverty – and these levels are understated since statistics take no account of the additional needs associated with either adult or child disability yet assume disability benefits are additional income. There is official commitment to increase the employment rate of disabled adults, and policies aim to deliver this. A recent Institute for Public Policy Research study suggested a million disabled adults wanted to work but were not doing so.[20] If these figures are true, and policies (for example, the supportive aspects of the Pathways to Work schemes) enable parents who are able and willing to take up work to do so, this is very welcome. However, such an aspiration should not mask the difficulties in terms of individual capacities, the existence of appropriate jobs, the willingness of employers to accommodate specific needs, or the level of disengagement from the labour market which may have occurred. Each of these issues needs to be addressed, and options that enable disabled adults to access work must be developed – not least the provision of affordable childcare (discussed below). Increasing the conditions associated with receipt of incapacity benefit to attempt to force parents into work would be neither socially just nor is this likely to bring about a fall in child poverty, since such a strategy may well result in low-paid, part-time, potentially unstable employment – it would prove to be a short-term saving to the Treasury but a cost to children in poverty.

A lack of available, affordable and suitable childcare is noted many times in this book. Government efforts[21] to improve the availability of childcare are important both in recognising the problem and more direct-ly improving provision, often least available in the poorest areas (offering the least profit to private providers) and inflexible (for example, to those working shift patterns). Government has partly recognised affordability problems through the childcare element of WTC and by proposing to increase the subsidy from 70 to 80 per cent (and capped by an amount, disadvantaging those with expensive needs, such as those with disabled children and those with larger families). Nevertheless, even after increas-ing the proportion of costs met, this will leave 20 per cent of costs requir-ing to be paid even by the poorest families in work. The numbers in receipt of the childcare credit are small (about 6.8 per cent of families with a tax credit award in July 2004[22]) and the targeting of the subsidy is not close-ly on the poorest families,[23] presumably mainly due to work criteria (all adults in a family having to be working for 16 hours or more). This disad-vantages parents who work fewer hours and those who may need help for other reasons – for example, disabled parents or those seeking work.

Structural discrimination in the labour market is also raised as a fac-tor in several of the chapters in this book and is most acutely demon-strated by the ban imposed on asylum seekers gaining paid work, which actively excludes families from increasing very low incomes in this manner. There is also structural discrimination in terms of where good jobs are located. This comes over strongly in Chapter 5 and links with the lower wage incomes that some minority ethnic groups typically receive. Issues of labour market and employer discrimination, in terms of pay and of opportunities, apply to many parents of the children under discussion in this book. The continuation of such a clear difference in the earnings of men and women has significant implications for children of lone parents who are overwhelmingly female.

The groups of children discussed in this book have most to gain from additional employment income, but paradoxically they have much to lose from some of the policy choices that have followed the focus on work. Children with parents for whom adequately remunerated work is an option and is delivered experience significantly lower rates of child pover-ty. But while the Government assumes policies intended to increase work effort will prove effective in continuing to reduce poverty for most families, the barriers discussed throughout this book challenge that view for some of the children most at risk of poverty. Indeed, work-focused social policy may threaten the groups of children described in this book, not just because they are clearly not benefiting equally from such a policy, but because they may be actively damaged by the negative rhetoric and policy choices which have accompanied it. Language such as Tony Blair's description of disability claimants 'languishing on benefits'[24] blames victims, exacerbating existing stigma for those not in work. The tough rhetoric is also associated with a raised profile of conditionality within social policy to strongly encourage people into jobs. If conditionality forces parents into unsuitable, poorly paid or unsustainable employment, it will not only fail to reduce child poverty, but it would be both socially unjust and counterproductive. The introduction of WTC aimed at increasing in-work incomes has been accompanied by the diminution of the adult rates of income support (IS), which have continued to fall in real terms under successive governments, not halted by the Labour Government's anti-poverty drive. One justification for the inadequacy of IS is the Government's determination to improve 'work incentives' by increasing the gap between in and out of work income. The consequence for children whose parents receive IS is a continued diminution of the real terms value of an already inadequate safety net.

Conclusion

Four brief points are worth ending on which draw out the key role of paid work in reducing child poverty as well as its limitations, and which sum up the direction of current policy:

- The broad direction of government policy in this area is right: the sustainable long-term solution to child poverty is greater employment income directed to families with children. However, this requires a greater equality of wages, brought about by skills investment and action to increase the real level of the minimum wage. While the Government is addressing these issues, a step change in the level of activity is required. For adults with low skill levels the challenge is especially significant – the employment levels shown in Figure 3.1 are reducing for this group. Successfully addressing this would have a significant benefit to both children and economic growth. The relation between low wages and poverty forms a circle. Low wages are a cause of inadequate income (and hence poverty) and since poverty is itself associated with poorer educational outcomes, poverty in childhood is also a cause of low adult wages. This is a vicious circle, transmitting disadvantage between generations – but it need not be so.

Intervention to improve education and training should provide a virtuous circle, improved parental labour market positions leading to greater equality of opportunity for children. The long-term solution is more labour market income, distributed more equally across the population. The short-term route to this is greater skills investment, and work to address educational disadvantage – led by the eradication of child poverty.

- Paid work is currently (nearly) the only route out of poverty – social assistance support is paid below the poverty line. The full benefit of paid work, in terms of protection of children from poverty, comes from having two parents in well-paid, full-time work. This is simply not available to all children: not all children have two parents living with them; not all children have parents able to work; and not all children have parents who can work full time. The expectation of parents working full time brings with it consequent costs in the time available for caring for children. It also ignores the unpaid element of work going on in families.

- To achieve greater increases in labour market income directed towards lower-income families, policy needs to address with greater urgency the structured discrimination that mars gains from the labour market. Later chapters discuss the spatial aspects, examining the impact on certain minority ethnic groups of their concentration in communities most affected by de-industrialisation, as well as the discrimination which persists not only in access to jobs but in access to good jobs. Issues of discrimination apply equally to the gender gap in pay, with its particular impacts on families reliant on the labour market income of a lone mother. Structural disadvantage requires structural responses to the labour market which include increasing targeted regeneration and greater efforts at rooting out discrimination in the labour market.

- Not all children will gain from current policy. Those who are most likely to lose are those currently at the greatest risk. There remains a need for other support, especially child benefit, to go alongside employment income in recognition of the additional costs children bring to families (while the benefits of them spread to society). An effective and adequate safety net is needed for those children whose parents' work options are limited to low-paid work, shorter hours or no paid work. Chapter 2 shows how far we are from that objective.

Notes

1   HM Treasury, *Child Poverty Review*, The Stationery Office, 2004

2   HM Government, *Department for Work and Pensions Five Year Strategy*, Department for Work and Pensions, 2005, Annex One, PSA Objective II

3   In 1997 it was at 72.7 per cent and has since risen to 74.7 per cent (as of the 2004 spring quarter, and defined in terms of working age adults), see National Statistics, *Labour Market Trends*, March 2005, Table A.1. Figures are for the UK.

4   Tony Blair MP, 'The Opportunity Society' speech at Beveridge Hall, University of London, 11 October 2004

5   National Statistics, *Labour Market Trends*, March 2005, Table A.4. Figures are for the UK.

6   HM Government, *Department for Work and Pensions Five Year Strategy*, Department for Work and Pensions, 2005, Annex One

7   Although the national minimum wage provides a floor for wages, in practice for most families entitlement to WTC would increase the net wage rate well beyond this

8   The marginal deduction rate refers to the combined impact of additional taxation and lower entitlement to benefits and tax credits on every additional pound of gross income earned; receipt of benefits and tax credits and tax liabilities will determine this. The picture is a complex one. A recent Treasury paper argues that reforms in the tax and benefit package (as it stood prior to the 1998 Budget and in 2005/06) have reduced the incidence of the highest marginal deduction rates, which is true if this is considered to be over 70p or more of each additional pound earned. However, the numbers facing a marginal deduction rate of 60p or more in the pound have increased by over 200,000 people (2.2 million facing rates of 60 per cent and above). See HM Treasury, *Tax Credits: reforming financial support for families*, HM Treasury, March 2005, para 4.20 and Table 4.3.

9   Although the provision of non-means-tested child benefit which redistributes income horizontally towards families with children implies the Government accepts society should help families above and beyond the income they can derive from the labour market

10 National Statistics, *Households Below Average Income, 1994/5–2003/04*, Department for Work and Pensions, 2005. Definition used is children living in households with equivalised incomes below 60 per cent of the national median income after housing costs.

11 DWP, *Measuring Child Poverty*, Department for Work and Pensions, 2003

12 National Statistics, *Households Below Average Income, 1994/5–2003/04*, Department for Work and Pensions, 2005

13 J Millar and K Gardiner, *Low Pay, Household Resources and Poverty*, Joseph Rowntree Foundation, 2004, p40

14 Making use of National Statistics, *Work and Worklessness among Households: time series*, available at www.statistics.gov.uk/statbase/Product.asp?vlnk= 12859&More=n, tables 3 (II), 3(III) and 3(IV)

15 Of 3.5 million children counted as income poor, 1.8 million had a parent in work. National Statistics, *Households Below Average Income, 1994/5–2003/04*, Department for Work and Pensions, 2005. Figures are for Great Britain.

16 C Howarth and P Kenway, *Why Worry about the Low Paid?*, New Policy Institute, 2004, Figure 5, p21

17 To see the combined effect of this with tax and other withdrawn entitlements see Department for Work and Pensions, *Tax Benefit Model Tables April 2004*, available at www.dwp.gov.uk/asd/asd1/TBMT_2004.pdf

18 National Statistics, *Households Below Average Income, 1994/5–2003/04*, Department for Work and Pensions, 2005, Table A2, p168

19 HM Government, *Skills: getting on in business, getting on at work*, Cm 6483-1, HMSO, March 2005

20 S Regan and K Stanley, *The Mission Million: supporting disabled people into work*, Institute for Public Policy Research, 2004

21 HM Treasury, *Choice for Parents, the Best Start for Children: a ten year strategy for childcare*, HMSO, 2004; CPAG has analysed this from a child poverty perspective, see *Child Poverty Action Group's Response to Choice for Parents, the Best Start for Children: a ten year strategy for childcare*, CPAG, 2005, available at www.cpag.org.uk

22 See Child Poverty Action Group manifesto, *Ten Steps to a Society Free of Child Poverty*, CPAG, 2005, p28

23 Demonstrated in modelling reproduced in Chapter 9 of the Institute for Fiscal Studies' *Green Budget* – see R Chote, C Emmerson, D Miles and Z Oldfield (eds), *The IFS Green Budget 2005*, Institute for Fiscal Studies, 2005

24 Used in a speech in Budapest, and reported by the BBC, *Benefit cuts 'to boost pensions'*, http://news.bbc.co.uk/1/hi/uk_politics/3745580.stm, 15 February 2004

Four

Children in acute housing need

Sue Regan and Jenny Neuburger

All I want is my own room. Then when I'm sick, I can just lie down and shut the door. (Ben, aged 10, with sickle cell disease)

We are seeing, in the classrooms, homeless children with lots and lots of emotional difficulties. They've been traumatised by the events that have happened, having moved from one place to the next. They're missing their family, and friends from schools. They're often reluctant to engage with adults as well, because of the fact they know they're going to be moving. (Sam Booth, Family Liaison Worker, Holy Name Primary School in Moss Side)

– From A Minton and S Jones, *Generation squalor: Shelter's national investigation into the housing crisis*, Shelter, 2005

Introduction

Children who are homeless and living in temporary accommodation or who are living in overcrowded conditions have difficult lives. Although young, they may have already undergone a traumatic life experience such as becoming homeless through domestic violence, or are living in cramped conditions where family relationships are put under strain and where it is impossible to find the space that is safe and quiet to play or do homework. In England alone, there were nearly 120,000 homeless children[1] living in temporary accommodation at the end of September 2004, and 900,000 children[2] living in overcrowded conditions – both closely associated with childhood poverty.

This chapter explores the experience of these children. We set out what is known about the numbers, distribution and impact of temporary accommodation and overcrowding, and describe the current policy context and progress that has been made in tackling these forms of housing need. We then disentangle the relationship between housing need and child poverty through using a simple conceptual framework, which leads us to a set of policy solutions.

We argue that the relationship between housing need and child poverty is not well understood by policy-makers, and that attempts to make further progress in tackling child poverty will be severely hampered if greater emphasis is not given to the role a safe, decent, affordable home plays in both preventing and providing a platform to escape poverty. Our solutions illustrate how public policy can do more to target specific negative interactions between housing need and child poverty. However, we conclude that a more comprehensive agenda is needed to tackle the root causes of homelessness and overcrowding, which recognises that a significant and sustained increase in public investment in social housing is central to this.

Children living in temporary or overcrowded accommodation are different from other groups of children described in this book, although crossover may be significant. Their common characteristic is their housing situation, which is a structural problem. The other groups of children are defined by a characteristic of themselves or their families, such as being disabled or from a black or minority ethnic community; or by their family's status, such as seeking asylum. While these characteristics can lead to greater risk of poverty due to indifference to their needs or directly discriminatory treatment, the aim is not to 'remove' their identifying characteristic. In contrast, for homeless families and those living in overcrowded accommodation, we want to remove the structural, common cause of their disadvantage. For poverty to be eliminated, all children must have a secure and suitable home.

The bigger picture on housing need

In relation to homelessness, focusing on the families and children living in temporary accommodation reveals only part of the homelessness picture. Over the calendar year 2004 nearly 300,000 households approached local authorities in England for help with their housing, of whom 200,000 were found to be homeless and 130,000 were found to be 'unintentionally homeless' and in priority need. Of this last group, half were families with children.[3] Families with children automatically have a priority need for housing within the legislation, but families who are deemed to have become 'intentionally' homeless are not accepted for re-housing by local authorities. Over 2004, approximately 13,600 households were found to be 'intentionally homeless', an increase of 175 per cent since 1997. Not all homeless households who local authorities accept are placed in temporary accommodation – around 21,000 are 'homeless at home'. In addition, all of these official figures fail to pick up households whose homelessness is 'hidden' because they have not approached a local authority for assistance – eg, people staying with friends or relatives, in direct access hostels or self-placed in bed and breakfasts. There are no reliable figures for this group.

There are also other forms of housing need which a focus on temporary accommodation and overcrowding excludes. The geographic distribution of these problems is broader than the use of temporary accommodation and overcrowding, which, as revealed in statistics below, tends to be concentrated in the South East of England, in particular London.

- Housing conditions: in 2001, nearly 500,000 children[4] lived in homes unfit for human habitation.
- Neighbourhood quality: in 2001, there were 2.4 million homes[5] in 'poor neighbourhoods'. The quality of neighbourhood is central to people's experience of home and to residential satisfaction, life chances and quality of life.
- Housing costs: in 2003/04, 2.6 million children counted as poor before housing costs (BHC) but 3.5 million counted as poor after housing costs (AHC).[6]

In relation to this latter category, the Government's decision to measure, as its headline poverty indicator, incomes *before housing costs* rather than *after housing costs* excludes these families poor on the latter but not on the former measure. The Government has stressed that these children will be captured by the new material deprivation indicator and will therefore still be counted as poor. It remains to be seen exactly how the new indicator will be constructed, and given the complex relationship between poverty and housing costs (discussed in more detail below), there is clearly a risk that these children will be lost to the official figures and their poverty not fully recognised.

This broader context illustrates the potential scope of the impact of housing need on child poverty. Temporary accommodation and overcrowding is worthy of particular attention owing to its scale and impact.

Children in temporary and overcrowded accommodation

Temporary accommodation

Although not literally on the streets, people living in temporary accommodation are homeless in every sense of the word – they have lost their home, often in very traumatic circumstances; have been 'officially' recognised as homeless by their local authority; and are forced to live in insecure and often inappropriate housing until a settled home can be found. During this time, they may be moved several times, causing severe disruption in terms of changing schools, access to the labour market and the loss of social and support networks which are associated not only with poverty but with transmitted deprivation.

By the end of September 2004, there were nearly 120,000 children[7] living in temporary accommodation (see Table 4.1 overleaf). The desperate shortage of council and housing association homes for rent means that local authorities are placing more and more homeless households in temporary accommodation. Half of this is accommodation leased from private landlords by local authorities or by housing associations on their behalf. Other forms of temporary accommodation include council and housing association properties let on a short-term basis. A fifth of temporary accommodation is hostels, bed and breakfast hostels and women's refuges in which people share toilets, bathrooms and kitchens.

Temporary accommodation is defined by being let on insecure tenancies (assured shorthold tenancies) or even less secure 'licenses'. Often temporary accommodation used by local authorities is outside the borough. For example, in London in March 2003, 15 per cent of households were placed in accommodation outside their borough – in Kensington and Chelsea, nearly half of households were placed in other boroughs.[8] Families have little or no control over their home environment and are often forced into frequent, unwanted moves between different temporary homes. Commonly, because the accommodation is contracted in, it is poorly regulated and managed and can be unsuitable and in poor condition. The combination of high rents and the structure of the housing benefit system mean that for many homeless households living in private sector temporary accommodation, working is not financially viable.

Since 1997 the number of households in temporary accommodation in England has more than doubled to over 100,000 households (66,000 families). Nearly two-thirds of households placed in temporary

Table 4.1

Homeless families with children in temporary accommodation, 2004

	Families with dependent children	Total number of children
England (Sept)	66,120	116,580
Scotland (Dec)	2,174	3,971
Wales (June)	1,449	2,608 *

* This figure is an estimate. It was calculated using 1.8 as the average number of dependent children per family and rounding to the nearest 10.

Source: Office of the Deputy Prime Minister P1E homelessness statistics, 2004

accommodation are in London, where shortages of social housing are concentrated. The term 'temporary' is a misnomer as the average length of time before getting a permanent home has almost trebled from an average of 98 days to an average of 267 days – and up to 381 days in London.[9]

Overcrowded accommodation

There are around 900,000 children living in overcrowded conditions in England and more than 100,000 living in severely overcrowded housing.[10] Again, the problem is concentrated in London where the worst housing shortages exist (see Table 4.2 opposite). In London's social housing, nearly one child in every three lives in an overcrowded home; it is little better in the private rented sector, where one child in every four lives in overcrowded conditions.[11] Although more overcrowded households live in the owner-occupied sector, due to the dominance of the sector, a larger proportion of households who rent live in overcrowded homes.

Groups affected

Many of the other groups of children described in other chapters in this book are disproportionately likely to be in overcrowded or temporary accommodation. For example, black and minority ethnic households are more than six times more likely than white households to be overcrowded.[12] Minority ethnic groups are also disproportionately likely to be homeless and living in temporary accommodation. However, studies have

Table 4.2

Families with children in overcrowded* homes, by region (average for each year 2000–03)

	Families with dependent children	Total number of children
England	361,800	905,000
North East	11,800	31,400
North West	46,700	123,800
Yorkshire and the Humber	32,400	86,000
East Midlands	21,900	57,900
West Midlands	36,700	97,300
East	26,600	70,400
London	118,700	261,000
South East	41,100	109,000
South West	25,800	68,200

*This is defined as lacking one or more rooms according to the bedroom standard.

Source: Office of the Deputy Prime Minister data from *Survey of English Housing 2000–2003* combined, figures rounded to nearest hundred. Figures for children in regions other than London are derived estimates and proportions are calculated using Census data.

shown that race is not itself a significant factor in causing homelessness, once other variables are controlled for.[13] It is only a further part of the disadvantage suffered in relation to incomes, work, tenure and area of residence.

Living in temporary accommodation also disadvantages children with disabilities or chronic health problems. This is due both to poor conditions and worse access to specialist health and other services. For example, accommodation is typically not designed to accommodate possible mobility problems of disabled people and social services do not provide aids and adaptations to families living in temporary accommodation.

Progress on housing and child poverty

The present Government is serious about ending child poverty. In 1999, the Prime Minister pledged to eradicate child poverty in a generation. A series of targets were announced – to end child poverty by 2020, to halve it by 2010 and to reduce it by at least a quarter by 2004/05. The main policy levers have been changes in taxes and benefits, the introduction of the minimum wage and initiatives to help parents back to work. Although the most recent *Households Below Average Income* figures reveal disappointing progress, throwing some doubt over whether or not the Government is on track to meet its first target,[14] progress has been made. Roughly 700,000 children have moved out of poverty, thanks largely to further increases in the generosity of tax credits.[15]

However, the approach so far has focused on work as a route out of poverty and on financial support for families. To make further progress, it is vital that a holistic view of child poverty is taken, including housing. The Work and Pensions Select Committee on child poverty in the UK acknowledged the role of housing, arguing for an indicator that continues to account for housing costs; for a housing needs indicator within the overall measure of child poverty; and for a higher earnings disregard before housing benefit is withdrawn.[16]

The Homelessness Act 2002 strengthened and increased the homelessness safety net. It included homeless 16- and 17-year-olds and people who are vulnerable due to fleeing violence, or leaving care, prison or the army among those whom local authorities have a duty to re-house. (Care leavers and children with parents in prison are discussed in greater detail in Chapters 12 and 9.) It replaced the duty (abolished under the Housing Act 1996) on local authorities to provide permanent housing, not just temporary accommodation for two years. It also placed general duties on local authorities to advise and assist all homeless people (whether or not they have a priority need for housing); to review homelessness in their local area; and to produce a strategy to tackle it.

On temporary accommodation, the Government set a target to end the long-term use of bed and breakfast hotels as temporary accommodation for families with children by April 2004. This target has been met. More recently, the Office of the Deputy Prime Minister's (ODPM's) *Five Year Plan*[17] contained a target to halve the number of homeless households living in temporary accommodation by 2010. It has published a strategy containing measures to achieve this target, mainly focusing on the role of homelessness prevention by local authorities to reduce acceptances and the flow into temporary accommodation. It also contained proposals to increase the use of the private rented sector and to examine the role of temporary-to-permanent housing initiatives, possibly legislating later in 2005. The increase in social house-building at current and planned levels is unlikely to mean that the target can be met through moving people onto permanent social housing.

While it is right that the Government has identified high levels of temporary accommodation as a problem which must be addressed, there is a danger that achieving this by moving people into or helping them sustain tenancies in the private rented sector – rather than providing affordable, secure homes – could fail to solve their problems and simply mean that they do not approach statutory services for help.

In the Housing Act 2004, the Government introduced an amendment giving a power to enable a new statutory definition of overcrowding to be set by regulations. The existing statutory definition (unlike the bedroom standard) has not been changed since its introduction in 1935 and failed to count babies under a year; counted those aged between one and ten years as half a person; and included kitchens and living rooms as places to sleep. At the time of writing, a consultation on the regulations was due to be published in 2005. Whether this new definition will be accompanied by a strategy to tackle overcrowding is not yet clear.

A conceptual framework for housing need and child poverty

Why does housing situation matter to child poverty? Why are homeless children in temporary accommodation and children in overcrowded housing among high-risk groups of poverty? There is a complex interaction between housing need and poverty, which we attempt to clarify through the conceptual framework below. The framework illustrates these different interactions: the coupling of housing need and poverty in its narrowest sense of 'lack of income'; between housing need and health and education, which influence the experience of poverty; and between housing and the experience of poverty in its widest sense of 'capability deprivation'[18] – ie, lacking the social, material and other resources (including housing) to live a full life. We explore four interactions in turn to examine the experience of children living in temporary accommodation and overcrowded conditions.

Housing need is a:
1. consequence of poverty;
2. cause of poverty;
3. contributor to poverty;
4. constituent of poverty.

This means that meeting housing need, and reducing homelessness and overcrowding, can be part of the solution to poverty and that solving other elements of poverty can contribute to reducing housing need.

1. Consequence of poverty

Housing need – whether this is homelessness or overcrowding – can be a result of poverty. The interaction between low income and housing need is negatively reinforcing. For example, the poorest fifth of the population are 1.4 times more likely than the rest of the population to be living in a 'non-decent' home, and are the most likely to be living in accommodation with less room.[19] Studies have shown that the likelihood of homelessness correlates very strongly with unemployment, low incomes and poverty.[20] For instance, family homelessness is normally the culmination of a series of problems such as low income, loss of employment, household debt, relationship breakdown and repossession for arrears. Because of a low income, families are unable to re-house themselves. As housing need can be a consequence of low income, then clearly reducing income poverty can lead to a reduction in homelessness and bad housing.

2. Cause of poverty

Different forms of housing need can cause poverty by reducing income through high housing costs or through barring access to employment. In 2003/04, 2.6 million children counted as poor BHC but 3.5 million counted as poor AHC.[21] The effects of high rents are particularly acute for homeless families placed in temporary accommodation.

Table 4.4
Barriers to work, training and education

	Household with children (number)	Household without children (number)
Health/mobility problems	22	54
Mental health problems	27	20
Lack of childcare	41	–
High rents mean cannot afford it	28	17
Worried about changes to benefits	25	20
Don't know how long I will be living here	13	13
Total number of responses	**143**	**87**

Source: Shelter temporary accommodation survey 2003

Impact of living in temporary accommodation on employment

Living in temporary accommodation for months, years in some cases, causes long-term exclusion from work. Findings from a Shelter survey of 2,000 homeless households living in temporary accommodation found that over 77 per cent of households – 71 per cent of families with children – had no household member in work. This compares to out-of-work rates of between 40 and 50 per cent among their counterparts – formerly homeless households – living in more affordable council or housing association homes. Over 90 per cent of households were receiving housing benefit to help cover their rent.[22]

The main barriers to work and training identified by families included: lack of childcare; health problems caused or exacerbated by living in temporary accommodation, particularly depression; and high rents in temporary accommodation (see Table 4.4).

> My rent is £125 per week and if I wanted to work then how on earth am I supposed to afford my rent when I will only probably earn around £100 to £150 per week?...[23]

> Before...I was working for the council, for social services as a home carer. I had a purpose in life and I was a living person. Now I am a nothing. I can't

work because I am so depressed and even if I did work, you know, how am I meant to cope…being in temporary accommodation one week you could be there, the next week you could be living somewhere else.[24] (Zoe)

This picture does not improve significantly over time. Households who had been living in temporary accommodation for more than a year still had lower rates of employment than they had before they became homeless, and also much lower than their counterparts in social housing.[25]

3. Contributor to poverty

Housing need is a contributor to poverty and can exacerbate the experience of poverty. In the example below, we look at how living in temporary or overcrowded accommodation can impact on the health and education of children.

Impact of temporary and overcrowded accommodation on health and education

The impacts of living in temporary and overcrowded housing on families' and children's health and education are very different, but equally debilitating.

Families and children in temporary accommodation

Families living in temporary accommodation interviewed by Shelter[26] felt that their health and that of their children had suffered in a number of ways since they became homeless and were placed in temporary accommodation. This included both the development of mental health problems, such as depression, and physical health problems, such as asthma caused by damp and condensation. Poor conditions and facilities are also a problem in temporary accommodation, particularly in shared bed and breakfast and hostel accommodation. A third of households in Shelter's survey reported damp and mould in their home and 38 per cent said that the cooking facilities were poor and unhygienic. For hostel dwellers these were more major concerns – 38 per cent and 58 per cent reporting these problems respectively. The risk of fire is much greater in bedsits, shared houses and hostels, which are used as temporary accommodation, than in self-contained flats and houses.[27] One study found that children living in bed and breakfast hostels were twice as likely to be admitted to hospital with burns and scalding.[28]

Families also explained how existing health problems worsened and were more difficult to manage in unsuitable and unfamiliar surroundings with poor access to health care and support. For example, one large family were moved into a small one-bedroom flat, which meant they were overcrowded. The son had autism and other family members had mobility and respiratory problems and there was no reliable lift service to the first-floor flat. The heating and hot water systems were faulty and the frequent change was worsening the son's autism.

> Every time we move it is not good for my son, because we have moved about two or three times and it disturbs him, you know what I mean, because of the change…because he doesn't know what's going on…his mental condition worsens.[29] (Sofia)

The results of Shelter's survey provided clear evidence of the negative impacts of living in temporary accommodation on the health of parents and children. Overall, half of people said that their health or their family's health had suffered due to living in temporary accommodation. The most alarming finding was the very high rates of depression: nearly half of parents reported being depressed, which clearly impacted on children. Forty-two per cent of parents said that their child was 'often unhappy or depressed'.

Children's education also clearly suffers. Frequent moving and disruption makes it difficult for children to keep school places, maintain attendance and do well at school. The loss of both home and school can be a double blow for homeless children, as their two most stable environments are gone. Shelter's survey showed that children had missed an average of 55 days of school over a year, equivalent to a quarter of the school year. Some did not have school places in a new area and many children faced long journeys to school and problems with transport when their temporary accommodation was outside their local area. Children who took part in a Shelter research project[30] described problems moving homes and schools, making new friends and being bullied.

> …for four months we didn't go to school, we went to six houses, no, seven houses and six new schools; …I don't like moving, because every time I make new friends and then I have to move again and again and again. (Girl, 10)

Families in overcrowded accommodation

Research into health outcomes associated with overcrowding concentrates on the hygiene risks, common mental health disorders and increased risk of accidents, as well as a number of other health impacts. Measles, mumps, chickenpox, diphtheria, and most respiratory conditions are more easily spread in crowded conditions, as are those spread through physical contact such as scabies. The tension and stress in an overcrowded environment can worsen existing health problems and often leaves parents, particularly mothers, suffering from anxiety and depression.

Living in cramped conditions can also affect children's educational attainment. Overcrowding can make it hard for children to find a quiet space to read or do their homework, which becomes even more acute for those sitting GCSEs or A levels. Children sharing bedrooms or sleeping in living rooms often have their sleep disrupted by other family members, particularly older siblings who may arrive home late after younger children's bedtime. These disrupted sleep patterns can mean they don't get the rest they need, all of which means they are more likely to fall behind in school. This adds to the stress parents feel, and increases mental health problems.[31]

4. Constituent of poverty

Housing need should also be viewed as an integral part of poverty. Below, we explore how the lack of a secure, decent home is part of the experience of poverty, an intrinsic element of poverty. The most recent Public Service Agreement target on reducing child poverty is based on a new multi-tiered approach to measuring child poverty.[32] This includes a measure of material deprivation which looks at socially perceived necessities that families and children lack, including a warm home, enough money to keep a home in a decent state of repair and enough bedrooms for children. This takes us towards a fuller measure of the experience of poverty, including the material aspects of housing need. However, it does not capture the social dimensions of poverty caused by the lack of a home.

The lack of a secure, decent home – impact on well-being

The lack of a permanent home with enough room and in an area with safe places to relax with friends is a key element of the deprivation that homeless and overcrowded children experience, even apart from the impacts on family income, health and education. Most people value a secure, decent home over which they have a degree of control and in an area where they are comfortable. For families and children, this is particularly important, as is contact with family, friends and other local support networks. The best way to explain this is through what children and families living in temporary and overcrowded conditions say.[33]

Overcrowding

> It is so small I have to share a room with my brothers. They are watching TV in my room while I am doing my homework. Younger children need more space because they want to explore places. Older children won't worry about staircases – they will want a place to do their homework. (Christopher, aged 14)

> …I want my own room where I can be organised. (Girl, 10)

Temporary housing: lack of control and insecurity

> It has affected me because…this uncertainty, you don't know what is happening tomorrow, and you are…upset…every time, maybe we will move. I am already in some uncertainty because of my son, and with temporary accommodation I don't know what will happen tomorrow. (Jo)

> Other people are deciding for me, for my son [we have] no choice. (Jo)

> It's torture, absolute torture, not knowing when you are going to be re-housed and where you are going to be re-housed. They are the two worst things I think. You are just constantly worried. When and where. (Zoe)

Leaving temporary housing: getting a permanent home

> I don't think, I know, that I would be able to get my life back, being placed in permanent. (Zoe)

> My cat's gone to Battersea, My cat is so good I love her…when we get a new house we'll get her back. (Girl, 4)

> I think my house is so cool, it wasn't something that I was going to expect, in my bedroom, it's the size that I wanted. (Girl, 10)

Solutions to housing need and child poverty

These four perspectives on the relationship between housing need and child poverty lead to a better understanding of how secure, affordable housing is entwined with tackling child poverty. In our examples, ending overcrowding and the use of temporary accommodation is a necessary prerequisite of tackling wider poverty.

Public policy can target specific negative interactions between living in temporary or overcrowded accommodation and worklessness, poor health or missing education, identified in this chapter. For example, three East London local authorities, together with the Greater London Authority and East Thames Housing Association, have created a 'Working Future' pilot project. The scheme is designed to remove barriers to work through reducing rents in temporary accommodation leased from private landlords down to the average charged by local social landlords – around £80 a week, instead of £300 a week. The gap will be met through a block grant paid direct to the local authority. Another positive initiative is NOTIFY, a London-wide notification system to improve access to health, education and social services for homeless families placed in different London boroughs. These interventions are valuable and necessary.

However, this approach is limited. As Pleace and Quilgars[34] argue in relation to the poor health of homeless people, the solution is not to improve access to health services but to reduce levels of homelessness. If homeless and overcrowded children are to have improved life chances and escape poverty, then we must ensure they are no longer homeless or overcrowded. As discussed earlier, the Government has recognised the scale and impact of being homeless and living in temporary accommodation and its Homelessness Strategy provides a useful framework for taking this forward. On overcrowding, the Government is much less committed. There was no reference to the problem of overcrowding in the ODPM's *Five Year Plan* but action may flow from its commitment to redefine the overcrowding standard.

Overall, if we are to tackle these two acute forms of housing need, a much more ambitious strategy is needed which builds on what the Government has done to date but takes it much further. This includes genuine homelessness prevention and advice and support to help people sustain their current homes. The children living in temporary accommodation are there because of the lack of permanent social housing. Numerous studies have shown that there is an acute shortage of social housing, particularly – but not exclusively – in areas of high housing demand. The recent ODPM Select Committee concluded:

> …the shortage of suitable, permanent low-cost housing is a fundamental cause of homelessness….A major building programme of low-cost permanent housing to rent is required for homeless people. The serious shortage of permanent housing for homeless people is causing long stays in temporary accommodation. It is unacceptable that homeless people should spend very long periods, sometimes several years, in hostels and other forms of temporary accommodation.[35]

Similarly, families are overcrowded because of lack of affordable, family sized homes.

The increase in social housing needed will require a range of approaches: better use of existing homes through schemes which encourage mobility away from high demand areas; increased use of 'temporary-to-permanent' schemes which over time increase the social housing stock; an emergency acquisition programme; but fundamentally it requires a significant and sustained increase in public investment to build new homes.

This necessary increase in social housing is most urgent for children living in temporary or overcrowded homes, but is also needed to tackle child poverty more widely.

Conclusion

The relationship between housing need and child poverty is not well understood by policy-makers, although recent government pronouncements have illustrated that this is improving. For example, the Social Exclusion Unit[36] recently flagged up homelessness as one of the five key challenges to improving life chances and tackling social exclusion. It is clear that attempts to make further progress in tackling child poverty will be severely hampered if greater emphasis is not given to the role a safe, decent, affordable home plays in both preventing and providing a platform to escape poverty.

Notes

1 Office of the Deputy Prime Minister P1E homelessness statistics, 2004
2 L Reynolds, N Robinson and R Diaz, *Crowded House: cramped living in England's housing*, Shelter, 2004
3 Office of the Deputy Prime Minister P1E homelessness statistics, 2004
4 This figure is an estimate. It was calculated using 1.8 as the average number of dependent children per family and rounding to the nearest thousand. Source: ODPM, *English House Condition Survey 2001*, Office of the Deputy Prime Minister, 2003.
5 ODPM, *English House Condition Survey 2001*, Office of the Deputy Prime Minister, 2003. For an overview of the relationship between housing and neighbourhood quality see ODPM, *Evaluation of English Housing Policy 1975–2000: Theme 3: housing quality and neighbourhood quality*, Office of the Deputy Prime Minister, 2005.
6 Poverty is defined as having an income below 60 per cent of the median income. The 'before housing costs' income measure includes welfare benefits to help with housing costs – ie, housing benefit and income support for mortgage interest – but does not deduct rent or mortgage payments. The 'after housing costs' income measure deducts rent, water rates, mortgage interest payments and other ground rent or service charges. The difference between poverty rates using these different income measures indicates that people on lower incomes pay relatively more for housing, driving them into poverty. National Statistics, *Households Below Average Income, 1994/5–2003/04*, Department for Work and Pensions, 2005.
7 Office of the Deputy Prime Minister P1E homelessness statistics, 2004
8 Greater London Authority, *Homelessness in London*, 48, GLA, July 2003
9 House of Commons, *Official Report*, 28 June 2004: col. 94W
10 Overcrowding is calculated according to the bedroom standard used by the Government in the *Survey of English Housing and English House Condition Survey*. This standard allocates a separate bedroom for each couple or single person aged 21 or over; each pair of adolescents aged 10 to 20 years of the same sex; and each pair of children under 10 years of age. Any unpaired person aged between 10 and 20 is paired if possible with a child under 10 of the same sex or, if that is not possible, is given a separate bedroom, as is any unpaired child under 10.
11 L Reynolds, N Robinson and R Diaz, *Crowded House: cramped living in England's housing*, Shelter, 2004

12 Ibid.

13 R Burrows, 'The social distribution of the homelessness experience', in R Burrows, N Pleace and D Quilgars (eds), *Homelessness and Social Policy*, Routledge, 1997

14 M Brewer, *Will the Government Hit Its Child Poverty Target in 2004–05?*, Institute for Fiscal Studies, 2004

15 These figures are for an after housing costs measure. Before housing costs, the fall has been 600,000 children.

16 House of Commons Work and Pensions Committee, *Child Poverty in the UK: Second Report of Session 2003–04, Volume 1*, The Stationery Office, 2004

17 ODPM, *Sustainable Communities: Homes for All, A Five Year Plan from the Office of the Deputy Prime Minister*, Cm 6424, Office of the Deputy Prime Minister, 2005

18 Amartya Sen has developed a framework for analysing poverty using the concept of capabilities. This defines poverty as 'capability deprivation', broadly meaning the lack of social, economic and political resources to lead a full life, beyond lowness of income. See A Sen, *Development as Freedom*, Oxford University Press, 1999

19 A decent home is one that provides a reasonable degree of thermal comfort and is not overcrowded, ODPM, *English House Condition Survey 2001*, Office of the Deputy Prime Minister, 2003

20 For example, see R Burrows, 'The Social Distribution of the Homelessness Experience in Homelessness', in R Burrows, N Pleace and D Quilgars (eds), *Homelessness and Social Policy*, Routledge, 1997

21 National Statistics, *Households Below Average Income, 1994/5–2003/04*, Department for Work and Pensions, 2005

22 D Radebe, J Neuburger, F Mitchell and A Rayne, *Living in Limbo: survey of households living in temporary accommodation*, Shelter, 2004

23 Respondent to Shelter's temporary accommodation survey

24 S Credland, H Lewis and D Radebe, *Sick and Tired: the impact of temporary accommodation on the health of homeless families*, Shelter, 2004

25 D Radebe, J Neuburger, F Mitchell and A Rayne, *Living in Limbo: survey of households living in temporary accommodation*, Shelter, 2004

26 S Credland, H Lewis and D Radebe, *Sick and Tired: the impact of temporary accommodation on the health of homeless families*, Shelter, 2004

27 DETR, *Fire Risk in Houses in Multiple Occupation: Research Report*, The Stationery Office, 1998

28 S Richman, P Roderick, CR Victor and T Lissauer, 'Use of Acute Hospital Services by homeless children', *Public Health,* 105:4, 1991

29 S Credland, H Lewis and D Radebe, *Sick and Tired: the impact of temporary accommodation on the health of homeless families*, Shelter, 2004

30 Z Mustafa, *Listen Up: the voices of homeless children,* Shelter, 2004

31 L Reynolds, N Robinson and R Diaz, *Crowded House: cramped living in England's housing*, Shelter, 2004

32 DWP, *Measuring Child Poverty: final conclusions*; Department for Work and Pensions, December 2003

33 All of the comments are taken from interviews with parents and children. See Z Mustafa, *Listen Up: the voices of homeless children*, Shelter, 2004; S Credland, H Lewis and D Radebe, *Sick and Tired: the impact of temporary accommodation on the health of homeless families*, Shelter, 2004.

34 N Pleace and D Quilgars, 'Health, homelessness and access to health care services in London', in R Burrows, N Pleace and D Quilgars (eds), *Homelessness and Social Policy*, Routledge, 1997

35 House of Commons, ODPM: Housing, Plannning, Local Government and the Regions Committee, *Homelessness: Third Report of Session 2004–05, Volume 1 – Report*, The Stationery Office, 2005, para 121

36 Social Exclusion Unit, *Breaking the Cycle: taking stock of progress and priorities for the future*, Office of the Deputy Prime Minister, 2004

Part two
Groups at particular risk of poverty

Five
Poverty among black and minority ethnic children
Gary Craig

Research has shown that the UK's minority ethnic groups as a whole are more likely to be in poverty than the population at large. This has a profound impact on the life chances of most black and minority ethnic (BME) children. The greater likelihood of poverty is the consequence of a number of factors including:

- higher than average unemployment levels: minority ethnic communities largely remain residentially concentrated in inner cities where recession and industrial restructuring have weakened or destroyed older industrial sectors;
- racism in the selection of people for jobs or redundancy;
- the greater likelihood of being in low-paid work:
- inadequate health and housing provision; *and*, more recently,
- restrictions on State financial help for refugees and asylum seekers.

The way these factors have played out in recent years in terms of access to the labour market has been demonstrated both by large-scale studies[1] and by smaller-scale qualitative studies.[2] We cannot, however, assume that the minority ethnic community experience of poverty can be extrapolated from that of the population at large. For example, household and age structures of different minority ethnic groups are diverse, and the profile of the UK minority ethnic population as a whole is considerably 'younger' than the white population. For example, birth rates for Bangladeshi and Pakistani communities – while lower than for their country of origin – are higher than for the UK population as a whole and much higher than for the UK white population. For those out of the labour market, research continues to demonstrate that access to benefits remains more difficult, with take-up of benefits lower for minorities in general than among the white UK population because of confusion about the system, cultural obstacles and the failure of the social security system to provide adequate help for minorities seeking access to benefits. This is in part because the Department for Work and Pensions (DWP) does not monitor uptake of certain benefits by ethnic group.[3] Extraordinarily, the DWP Sixth Annual Report[4] has no analysis whatsoever – apart from a brief mention of Gypsy and Traveller children – of the Department's work in relation to minority ethnic children (see also Chapter 11 on Gypsy and Traveller children). This is an astonishing omission, given the connection between childhood experiences of poverty, and their opportunities and achievement in later life.

Geographical distribution of BME populations

Research also increasingly tells us that the UK's ethnic minorities – now numbering, as at the 2001 census, about 4.5 million, or 8 per cent of the UK population – are marked as much by diversity and difference within and between particular minority groups as by their common experience of racism (both individual and institutional) and discrimination. This minority population is unevenly distributed across the UK, with two-thirds of it concentrated in four English regions (London, East and West Midlands, and Yorkshire and the Humber) and more than two out of five minority members living in London alone.

Within the BME population, this geographical distribution also varies: for example, there is a greater proportion of Pakistanis living in Yorkshire and the Humber and in the West Midlands than in London. This geographical concentration is also reflected within regions with, for example, the Pakistani population in Bradford concentrated in the area of Manningham and Heaton and Leeds' Bangladeshi population largely living in Hunslet, all areas generally of declining older terraced houses and with deteriorating local labour market opportunities. This has implications for the development of faith schools since, in these areas, a number of schools have substantial numbers of minority ethnic children, particularly of Muslim religious orientation. Despite a concentration of minority children in certain schools, local minority faith organisations and Muslim populations in particular do not feel that these mainstream schools adequately address issues of religion. There are as yet only two Muslim State-aided schools. Faith schools are seen as one way of both protecting religious identity and encouraging educational achievement among minority children.[5]

Generational factors

It is also important to remember that about 40 per cent of the UK's minority ethnic population were actually born in the UK. As Atkin et al.[6] remind us, this results in important differences of an inter-generational kind, with differing attitudes, norms and dress. Also, for the UK-born of this population, educational, social and economic expectations and achievements are in general rather better than for those newly arrived in this country, of whatever generation, or those of their parents' or grandparents' generations who may have arrived as much as 50 years ago.

Refugees and European enlargement

The diversity within the UK BME population has grown in recent years, in part because of the large numbers of refugees arriving in Britain in the past 20 years (which has brought a range of ethnic groups – such as Afghani, Kurdish, Kosovan, Somali, Iraqi and Iranian – of which the UK had a relatively small number prior to the 1980s). This is also a result of European enlargement, which has introduced a growing number of migrant workers from countries such as Latvia, Hungary, Poland and the Czech Republic. This group has had relatively little impact at present on the numbers of minority children as they have tended to be single young workers, but there will be an impact over time as many of them partner and have children here.

Economic and social variations

Research[7] has also shown that there is considerable difference between the various UK minorities in terms of economic and social indicators. In general terms, people of Chinese and Indian origin tend to do better than the average (and than the white UK population) in terms of economic and educational achievement, those of Bangladeshi and Pakistani rather worse, with people of Black African and African-Caribbean origin exhibiting a less clear-cut pattern. Unemployment among African-Caribbean young men has consistently been much higher than the national average,[8] reflecting their much higher rate of permanent school exclusions than their white peers.[9] Within what are still widely regarded as single ethnic groupings, there may be marked differences; for example, research on the UK's Turkish population shows how there is a hierarchy between the three groupings of mainland Turks, Cypriot Turks and Kurdish Turks, in terms of educational attainment.[10]

Gender also, as we shall see, has an important impact; women of African-Caribbean origin have a much higher labour market participation rate than women in general, which has implications for childcare issues. Barely a quarter of African-Caribbean respondents to Middleton and Ashworth's survey of children's lifestyles[11] were able to use grandparents to provide childcare (compared with about 70 per cent of South Asian families and 50 per cent of white families). This also has impacts in terms of disposable income, since many families still pay a substantial proportion of their income on childcare. The Fourth National Survey of Ethnic Minorities[12] found that African-Caribbean women not only had the lowest level of free childcare and used childminders relatively more than any other ethnic group, but those using childcare paid for all or some of their childcare at a rate (58 per cent) almost twice that of the next highest scoring group. These patterns are slowly changing, however and, for example, the extended family form previously typical of many families of South Asian origin is now rather less common than hitherto, just as women in South Asian families are more active in the labour market than they were 10 years ago.

Family structure

Family structure is another important variable affecting the context for child-rearing and support. Seventy per cent of South Asians are married but only 20–25 per cent are single, compared with proportions of roughly 35 per cent (single) and 35 per cent (married) respectively for those of African-Caribbean origin.[13] Unpacking the category of South Asian, which covers at least four ethnic groupings defined in terms of national origins and substantially larger numbers of religious groupings, we find that Pakistani and Bangladeshi families with dependent children had more children and were more likely to live in larger households. Fifty-nine per cent of Pakistani and 65 per cent of Bangladeshi households consisted of five or more people (see Chapter 8 on larger families), compared with

8 per cent for white and 29 per cent for Indian families.[14] However, there are certain areas of family life, such as divorce, where we have relatively little data which can be analysed in terms of ethnicity. Given the impact that divorce may have in terms of increasing the risk of poverty for both reconstituted families, this is an important area yet to be explored, as is the issue of fatherhood. Strikingly, given the continuing myth surrounding South Asian families that 'they look after their own', a myth which still affects policy-making and service delivery, the 1999 *Health Survey for England*[15] found that substantially greater proportions of Indian, Pakistani, Bangladeshi and Chinese families all reported a severe lack of support than was the case with English and African-Caribbean populations.

Recent research

How does this general picture play out in relation to children of minority ethnic origin? It is worth observing that a detailed analysis is still not possible in some areas because of the lack of adequate data, particularly in areas with relatively small minority populations where it remains the case that public agencies still fail to take the issue of ethnicity seriously or have only recently begun to focus on it[16] – and much of what we know still relies on relatively small-scale qualitative research. Many organisations still do not monitor their data effectively in terms of ethnicity despite the fact that, at least for public bodies, ethnic monitoring is one of the critical tools underpinning the legal requirements of the Race Relations Amendment Act 2000, to promote racial equality and eliminate unlawful racial discrimination. Large-scale surveys also still do not achieve adequate samples of certain minority groups whose situation remains unexplored.

The large-scale survey and secondary analysis of other data sets undertaken by Gordon and colleagues,[17] however, points to the broad brush picture of poverty among minority ethnic children compared with their white counterparts. This survey was not able to distinguish between minorities because of the low numbers represented in the survey sample but concluded that, in relation to a list of socially defined necessities (eg, a damp-free home, a refrigerator, three meals a day for children), the proportion of children living in families lacking one or more items was almost twice as high for 'non-white' families as it was for white families, and for those lacking two or more necessities it was two and a half times as high (at 35 per cent) for 'non-white' families as it was for white families. Given the kinds of difference between minorities outlined above, there can be no doubt that these figures will show an even greater disparity in relation to certain minority group families with children; and given the association of poverty in general with low income, there can be little doubt that asylum-seeker children will be particularly badly off as their families are entitled only to an income substantially below that of normal income support levels. Their situation, and the dire position of destitute asylum seekers whose application for status has been rejected, is addressed more fully in Chapter 7. Having a large number of children within families has been associated historically, since the early days of Rowntree's research, with a greater risk of poverty: the *Health Survey for England* tells us that 47 per cent and 43 per cent respectively of Bangladeshi and Pakistani households had three or more children compared with 16 per cent for both white and African-Caribbean populations[18] (the *Fourth National Survey of Ethnic Minorities*[19] puts the gap between these groupings even larger).

We also know from this survey that Bangladeshi and Pakistani populations were much more likely at the time of the survey – at 42 per cent and 39 per cent respectively – to suffer from unemployment than other groups: the corresponding figures for white and Indian populations, for example, were 15 per cent and 19 per cent. The impact of this means that the former will have lower family incomes (£203 compared with £343 for the white UK population) and, because of family size, more demands upon these incomes. This explains the lack of necessities discussed in *Poverty and Social Exclusion in Britain*[20] and referred to above, a finding confirmed by the Small Fortunes national survey[21] a few years earlier; this showed that South Asian families were much more likely to indicate that they could not give their children all they wanted to compared with the UK white population.

It is not possible in this chapter to review all the evidence available regarding childhood poverty among BME children, even though this information is still relatively scarce compared with that of UK children as a whole. In the remainder of this chapter we focus on two aspects of childhood experience for BME children, that of the educational system and (very briefly) of social care.

Education

The overall picture in relation to the educational system is that, for most minorities, disadvantage and discrimination are still built into the system from a very early age. Despite the fact that each of the main minority ethnic groups has achieved higher standards than ever before, and indeed some are achieving rather better than the average, a report commissioned by OfSTED[22] found that BME pupils are disadvantaged systematically by the education system.

The issue is not simply an issue of the educational disadvantage associated with poverty – although that is powerful – but of the 'impact of policies, practice and procedures within schools and the wider educational system'.[23] Most strikingly, the OfSTED researchers concluded 'that any ethnic group could enter school 20 percentage points in advance of the average but leave it 21 points behind opens up an important educational debate on ethnic minority attainment', a finding as noteworthy for its profound understatement as for the deeply depressing facts it reports. 'In one large urban authority, African-Caribbean children entered school as the highest-achieving group but left as the group least likely to attain five high-grade GCSEs'.[24]

It has taken the effective refusal of certain groups to have their children educated within the predominantly white school system (through the establishment of single faith schools) to get government to acknowledge the need for sensitivity towards culture and religion within certain minority groups. In Bradford, a demographic analysis which looked at school rolls identified more than 500 Muslim girls as 'missing' (ie, effectively withdrawn) from state schools, reflecting the concern of parents for appropriate schooling for their daughters.[25] In fact, lack of understanding of why this cumulative disadvantage occurs can be traced back in part to the failure to engage in effective ethnic monitoring; this was argued for by the Rampton report in 1981 but still had not been put in place by 2000 in, according to one estimate, more than one in 200 schools. In many schools, despite the legal requirement on schools now both specifically to monitor pupils for ethnicity, and the more general requirements of the Race Relations Amendment Act 2000, it is clear that 'there remain considerable uncertainties around the recording of pupils' ethnic background':[26] some record one Black group, some two, some three, for example.[27]

Educational achievement among minorities, however, is variable, again reflecting the different general pattern of achievement between minority groups. Pupils of Indian origin had the best GCSE results in 1998 (with 66 per cent of girls and 54 per cent of boys achieving five or more GCSEs, grade A*–C, in 1999) compared with 55 per cent for white girls, 45 per cent for white boys but 37 per cent for Pakistani/Bangladeshi girls and 22 per cent for Pakistani/Bangladeshi boys. The comparable figures for Black girls and boys were 46 per cent and 31 per cent respectively, showing a much better rate across all minority groups for girls compared with boys. However, for Black and African-Caribbean boys in particular, the picture becomes even worse as they move through school. Rates of permanent exclusions for African-Caribbean boys, Black African and Black Other were at 75, 30 and 55 per 10,000 pupils respectively compared with a figure of 18 for white and less than half that for Indian pupils, figures which are a product as much of racism within schools as of the 'disruptive' behaviour of pupils (the latter itself often reflecting a cultural dissonance between pupil and teacher and low expectations by teachers of certain minority groups).[28]

More recent data[29] shows Chinese and Indian origin pupils outstripping all other groups (at 72 per cent and 64 per cent respectively compared with 51 per cent for all ethnic groups) but with the gap between Black groups and all other groups widening. Here, commentary on the data suggests that the variations in achievement are clearly linked to the fact that some groups are more likely to live in disadvantaged areas, with poor housing, poor schools and parents of lower social class (for example, using take-up of free school meals as a proxy for class: over 30 per cent of Pakistani and Black pupils and over 50 per cent of Bangladeshi pupils receive free school meals, substantially higher figures than the average for white pupils).

Research also demonstrates that minority ethnic pupils, and particularly those at schools where they are in a significant minority, suffer the effects of continuing racism from other pupils, and that teachers in the latter schools had had little or no training for dealing with issues raised by multicultural school populations.[30]

Probably the most comprehensive review of the position of minority children as they pass through school is the analysis of published data undertaken by Gillborn and Mirza.[31] Hopefully, their analysis indicated that 'of the six minority ethnic categories … analysed, every one [including Black groups] is the highest attaining of all in at least one LEA' – ie, that there is nothing culturally or educationally specific to any one group which dooms them always to fail in educational terms. However, the general picture is far less rosy. It may be the case that all ethnic groups have shared in the overall rise in educational attainment over the decade to 1997, for example, but the rate of improvement is roughly the same in all groups – leaving the gap between the better-achieving groups (Indian and white) and other, less well-achieving groups (particularly Black, Pakistanis and Bangladeshi) the same as it was at the beginning of the decade. Gillborn and Mirza observe that 'the familiar association between class and attainment can be seen to operate within [and between] each of the main ethnic groups'. Although there remains a gender gap, with girls outperforming boys, this is far less significant than the gaps associated with ethnic origin and class background. They conclude that:

> inequalities of attainment in GCSE examinations place African-Caribbean, Pakistani and Bangladeshi pupils in a disadvantaged position in the youth education, labour and training markets [including, more recently, the New Deal[32]], and increase the likelihood of social and economic exclusion in later life.

This plays out in differing ways: African-Caribbean and other Black groups are more likely than most others not only to be excluded from school but to disappear from official public view altogether.[33] Bangladeshi young people are more likely to move from GCSEs to GNVQ or vocational qualifications than aim for higher education, because of the cumulative effect of (mis-)education on their self-esteem, and this places them at a further disadvantage compared with their peers in terms of educational and economic opportunities as they enter adulthood. Interestingly, data from the Youth Cohort Study[34] also suggests that 'young people from ethnic minority groups are more likely to be in post-16 full-time education than white young people', but this may be as much a reflection for some groups of a reluctance to enter what is perceived to be a labour market still strongly structured by racism. Other research suggests that, as well as the more obvious impacts of poverty and disadvantage generally (and its effect on parental aspirations), length of settlement (which will affect recent migrants, and refugees and asylum seekers in particular),[35] fluency in English, teacher expectations and institutional racism all have an impact on young people's ability to achieve at school.[36] These factors all have a strong association with levels of poverty.

Social care

Finally, in relation to social care, the situation remains fairly uneven at best. A recent report from the Social Exclusion Unit has noted that children from minority backgrounds are less likely to access childcare and nurseries.[37] Consultation by the Daycare Trust with minority parents found again that childcare services were 'insensitive to the differing needs and perceptions of ethnic (sic) communities',[38] with some parents reporting outright racism.

The Social Services Inspectorate suggested five years ago that social services departments were failing minority ethnic children and families because of failure to recruit appropriate staff, to understand minority families' needs, and to implement equal opportunity policies. This is significant because of the continuing association between being in care and poor educational outcomes, and the greater likelihood that some minority groups such as African-Caribbean and other Black groups will be 'looked after' or have effectively disappeared from contact with official education, training and labour market agencies. The situation of minority young people being 'looked after' has yet to be explored in any great detail, 'a fact of which the policy and research community should not be particularly proud'.[39] National Voice, an advocacy organisation for children in and leaving care, supported by the Race Equality Unit, has also argued that young people experience racism within the care system and that social services have been failing BME children for years.

One small study has shown how young carers of Asian origin received little support from social services because of cultural stereotypes (see also Chapter 10 on disabled parents). Minority families actually have argued for social services support for them being mainstreamed into social services provision; this particular report suggesting that parents of South Asian origin had little confidence in the ability of social services to respond effectively to their particular cultural needs when specific ethnically-targeted services were provided.[40]

In response, social services departments have argued that for refugee children in particular, they have inadequate resources even to meet the basic requirements of the Children Act 1989. Here the government is not blameless, as the UK remains free to ignore the terms of the 1990 UN Convention on the Rights of the Child, the Major Government having demanded an opt-out in relation to caring for refugee children. None of the succeeding New Labour governments have argued for rescinding that provision.

In relation to carers, the National Black Carer Workers Network argues that service providers have failed to take account of race and culture in assessment, service provision – including interpretation – and funding. Family members are often called upon inappropriately to translate for social services staff. As with many other large public organisations, the impact of institutional racism is significant in shaping the way in which services are delivered: only one of the 180 social services departments in the UK currently has a black or minority ethnic director and most departments have abolished their race equality units over the past 10 years. As a result, while about 5 per cent of social services staff in 2000 were from minorities, that figure dropped to about 1.4 per cent in social services management, and policy and strategy was consequently less likely to be sensitive to the needs of minorities than if a significant proportion of senior managers had themselves been from minority backgrounds.

This picture is a profoundly worrying one. It points to the need for much more effective and reliable research on the needs of minorities to inform policy-making and service delivery – much research still has no effective 'race' dimension[41] and research funders should refuse to fund research which has no such dimension. It suggests that public bodies – including key government departments – need to incorporate ethnic monitoring more effectively into their ongoing data collection procedures, and act upon the findings of such monitoring. And it implies that a much more effective and coordinated strategy is required to address racism within the welfare system. Properly implementing the terms of the Race Relations Amendment Act would be a good start, but just that – a start.

Acknowledgement: I would like to acknowledge a debt of gratitude to Victoria Allgar of the University of Leeds, whose work on ethnicity and parenting made writing parts of this chapter rather easier than they might otherwise have been.

Notes

1 For example, Cabinet Office, *Ethnic Minorities and the Labour Market*, Cabinet Office Strategy Unit, 2003

2 For example, G Craig, H Dietrich and J Gautie, 'Excluded youth or young citizens? Ethnicity, young people and the labour market in three EU countries', in J Hoof and H Bradley (eds.), *Young People, Labour Markets and Social Citizenship*, Policy Press, 2005

3 See, for example, G Craig, 'Citizenship, exclusion and older people', *Journal of Social Policy*, January 2004; N Finch and P Kemp, *The Use of the Social Fund*

by Families with Children, In-house Report 139, Department for Work and Pensions, 2004; NAO, *Helping Those in Financial Hardship: the running of the social fund*, HC 179, National Audit Office, 2005

4 DWP, *Opportunity for All*, *Sixth Annual Report*, Cm 6239, Department for Work and Pensions, 2004

5 See R Penn, 'British population and society in 2025: some conjectures', *Sociology*, 34, 2000, pp5–18

6 K Atkin, WIU Ahmad and L Jones, 'Young South Asian deaf people and their families: negotiating relationships and identities', *Sociology of health and illness*, 24:1, 2001, pp21–45

7 For example, T Modood, R Berthoud, J Lakey, J Nazroo, P Smith, S Virdee and S Beishon, *Ethnic Minorities in Britain: diversity and disadvantage – Fourth National Survey of Ethnic Minorities*, Policy Studies Institute, 1997

8 L Britton, B Chatrik, B Coles and G Craig, *Missing Connexions?*, Policy Press, 2001

9 G Palmer, J North, J Carr and P Kenway, *Monitoring Poverty and Social Exclusion*, 2003, New Policy Institute, 2003

10 P Enneli, H Bradley and T Modood, *Young Turks?*, Policy Press, 2005

11 S Middleton and K Ashworth, *Small Fortunes: national survey of the lifestyles and living standards of children*, CRSP, University of Loughborough, 1995

12 T Modood, R Berthoud, J Lakey, J Nazroo, P Smith, S Virdee and S Beishon, *Ethnic Minorities in Britain: diversity and disadvantage – Fourth National Survey of Ethnic Minorities*, Policy Studies Institute, 1997

13 JCLR, *National Child Development Study 2000 and 1970 British Cohort Study Follow-Ups*, University of London, 2000

14 B Erens, P Primatesta and G Prior (eds), *Health Survey for England 1999: the health of minority ethnic groups*, Department of Health, The Stationery Office, 2001; see also L Platt, *Parallel lives?*, CPAG, 2002

15 B Erens, P Primatesta, G Prior (eds), *Health Survey for England 1999: the health of minority ethnic groups*, Department of Health, The Stationery Office, 2001

16 See U Brown, G Scott, G Moooney and B Duncan (eds), *Poverty in Scotland*, CPAG, 2002; A Darr, K Atkin and G Craig, *Ethnic Minorities in a Rural Labour Market*, North Yorkshire Learning and Skills Council and Universities of Hull and Leeds, 2004

17 D Gordon, R Levitas, C Pantazis, D Patsios, S Payne, P Townsend, L Adelman, K Ashworth, S Middleton, J Bradshaw and J Williams, *Poverty and Social Exclusion in Britain*, Joseph Rowntree Foundation, 2000

18 B Erens, P Primatesta and G Prior (eds), *Health Survey for England 1999: the health of minority ethnic groups*, Department of Health, The Stationery Office, 2001

19 T Modood, R Berthoud, J Lakey, J Nazroo, P Smith, S Virdee and S Beishon, *Ethnic Minorities in Britain: diversity and disadvantage – Fourth National Survey of Ethnic Minorities*, Policy Studies Institute, 1997

20 D Gordon, R Levitas, C Pantazis, D Patsios, S Payne, P Townsend, L Adelman, K Ashworth, S Middleton, J Bradshaw and J Williams, *Poverty and Social Exclusion in Britain*, Joseph Rowntree Foundation, 2000

21 S Middleton and K Ashworth, *Small Fortunes: national survey of the lifestyles and living standards of children*, CRSP, University of Loughorough, 1995

22 D Gillborn and H Mirza, *Educational Inequality: mapping race, class and gender*, Institute of Education and Middlesex University, 2000

23 DfES, *Aiming High: raising the achievement of ethnic minority pupils*, Department for Education and Skills, 2003

24 J Flaherty, J Veit-Wilson and P Dornan, *Poverty: the facts*, 5th edition, CPAG, 2004

25 S Simpson, 'Demography and ethnicity: case studies from Bradford', *New Community*, 23(1), 1997, pp89–107

26 T Cline, G de Abreu, C Fihosy, H Gray, H Lambert and J Neale, *Minority Ethnic Pupils in Mainly White Schools*, DfES Research Brief No. 365, Department for Education and Skills, 2002

27 D Gillborn and H Mirza, *Educational Inequality: mapping race, class and gender*, Institute of Education and Middlesex University, 2000

28 See, for example, R Cohen, *School Exclusions*, Barnardos, 1996; SEU, *School exclusion and truancy*, Social Exclusion Unit, 1998; L Sukhnandan and B Lee, *Streaming, Setting and Grouping by Ability*, National Foundation for Educational Research, 1998; data from Department for Education and Employment, First Statistical Release, National Statistics, 1989

29 T Cline, G de Abreu, C Fihosy, H Gray, H Lambert and J Neale, *Minority Ethnic Pupils in Mainly White Schools*, DfES Research Brief No. 365, Department for Education and Skills, 2002

30 Ibid.

31 D Gillborn and H Mirza, *Educational Inequality: mapping race, class and gender*, Institute of Education and Middlesex University, 2000

32 J Flaherty, J Veit-Wilson and P Dornan, *Poverty: the facts*, 5th edition, CPAG, 2004

33 L Britton, B Chatrik, B Coles and G Craig, *Missing Connexions?*, Policy Press, 2001

34 www.statistics.gov.uk/STATBASE/Product.asp?vlnk=10097

35 But not necessarily: one asylum seeker child known to the author arrived in the UK four years ago speaking no English; at the time of writing she was awaiting her A level results to see whether she could take up an offer to study at Cambridge

36 DfES, *Aiming High: Raising the achievement of ethnic minority pupils,* Department for Education and Skills, 2003

37 Social Exclusion Unit, *Tackling Social Exclusion*, Office of the Deputy Prime Minister, 2004

38 *Community Care*, 17 October 2003

39 L Britton, B Chatrik, B Coles and G Craig, *Missing Connexions?*, Policy Press, 2001

40 NFPI, *South Asian Hindus and Muslims in Britain – developments in family support*, National Family and Parenting Institute, 2003

41 G Craig and S Katbamna, '"Race" and social research', in S Becker and A Bryman, *Understanding Social Research*, Policy Press, 2004

Six
Disabled children
Ruth Northway

The early years of life are a 'critical period' for all disabled children, affecting both their development and their life chances.[1] Despite this, the Government acknowledges that they are still more likely to live in poverty than their non-disabled peers, and that to meet Government targets of halving child poverty by 2010, and eliminating it by 2020, specific action targeted at disabled children and their families will be required.

This chapter will thus:

- explore the relationship between disability, poverty and social exclusion;
- examine both the causes and effects of poverty among disabled children and their families;
- review the recommendations for change set out in key reports and research;
- compare these to the actions currently proposed by the Government;
- make recommendations for further action required.

It is acknowledged that a number of research studies and reports have been published concerning this topic. In this chapter, however, the focus will primarily be on recent publications and policy developments since these both build upon and extend existing knowledge.

Disability, poverty and social exclusion

It is difficult to obtain clear statistics as to how many disabled children there are currently within the UK. There are a number of reasons for this. First, there are a number of different approaches to determining who might be considered to be disabled. For example, one measure might be the number of children in receipt of disability related benefits. However, as will be seen later in this chapter this is likely to be an underestimate due to underclaiming of benefits. A second approach might be to use the number of children accessing services provided for disabled children. This is also unlikely to give a true picture since eligibility criteria for services may be dependent upon having certain diagnoses which children may not have (despite having particular needs). Another reason for the difficulties experienced in determining the numbers of disabled children can be use of the term 'disabled', since parents may not view their child as being disabled but rather as having 'special needs'.[2] They may thus be loath to accept such a label which will mean that their children may not appear in statistics.

Despite these difficulties the Government states that there are 770,000 disabled children in the UK and that while older people are more likely to be disabled than younger people, the largest rise in the incidence of disability over the past 30 years has been among children.[3] These figures appear to be based upon the results of the 2002 *General Household Survey*[4] and suggest that disabled children are a growing and significant group within UK society.

Almost all disabled children now live at home with their families. Between 17,500 and 20,000 families are providing care for more than one disabled child and over 15,000 severely disabled children are living in families where there is at least one other severely disabled child.[5]

Not all disabled children will experience poverty but they are more likely than their non-disabled peers to live in poverty.[6] Gordon et al.[7] have used a widely accepted definition of poverty to calculate that, in 1985, almost 55 per cent of families in Britain with a disabled child were living either in poverty or at its margins. Sharma[8] found that although there had been changes in the system of disability benefits, disabled children and young people were still more vulnerable to poverty. Those who live in lone-parent families and those from black and minority ethnic families are at particular risk.[9] Families of disabled children may thus also experience other factors which increase vulnerability to poverty, as discussed elsewhere in this book.

Poverty can also be seen as a cause of disability. Poor maternal nutrition and poor nutrition for neonates can give rise to childhood disability,[10] mild to moderate learning disability is linked to poverty with incidence rates being higher in urban areas,[11] and children of parents in manual occupation groups have a higher risk of serious childhood illness and disability.[12]

Alcock,[13] however, argues that poverty is not an inevitable consequence of disability but rather that it results from a failure of society to respond appropriately to the needs of disabled people. He thus states that it is discrimination rather than disability itself which leads to the poverty and social exclusion of disabled people. This view is in keeping with a social rather than an individual model of disability. The latter would argue that disability is a characteristic of the individual who is unable to take a full role in society due to her/his inability to do certain things. A social model, however, states that while people do have impairments (and may require some support with these impairments), what disables them is a range of barriers which prevents their full participation in society. Disability is thus something which is imposed on individuals by a failure of society to identify and remove barriers. In this context a lack of financial resources is one such barrier which prevents participation.

Such a view also moves poverty beyond consideration of just the financial resources available to individuals and their families and leads to acknowledgement of the consequences of poverty for disabled children and their families. Social exclusion is viewed as the 'circumstances of deprivation and disadvantage that extend beyond lack of material resources'.[14] As will be seen in this chapter, many disabled children and their families experience such social exclusion as a result of a failure to acknowledge and meet their additional needs. Material circumstances and social exclusion are thus linked.

The causes and effects of poverty

While accepting that poverty should not be an inevitable consequence of disability, there are two key factors which contribute to the poverty experienced by disabled children and their families: vulnerability to reduced incomes often derived from social security benefits and the impact of additional disability related costs.

Reduced incomes

Work is viewed as the most important (but not guaranteed) route out of poverty for those of working age.[15] Nonetheless, while some parents of disabled children do continue to work, many give up paid employment in order to provide care for their disabled child(ren). The reasons for this are varied and include inflexible employers, difficulties with suitable and affordable childcare, fears about losing benefits, the child's ill health, and medical appointments.[16] In addition, time away from the workplace to provide care can have long-term consequences in terms of missed opportunities for promotion and career development. Where parents do seek to rejoin paid employment they may find themselves offered work which is low paid and often below their level of training/qualifications.[17]

Families of disabled children are thus often reliant upon social security benefits as their major or sole source of income. However, many parents do not receive the level of benefits to which they are entitled due to a lack of information concerning such benefits and difficulties with making applications.[18] This is particularly the case for families from black and minority ethnic groups[19] (see Chapter 5).

In the study undertaken by Preston[20] some families mentioned a reluctance to be on benefits due to stigma and also due to the fact that they did not perceive their child to be 'disabled'. However, they also reported difficulties with obtaining the necessary forms, filling them in, submitting subsequent claims (some benefits being awarded for specific periods of time) and dealing with appeals. Disability living allowance (DLA) was viewed as being 'notoriously difficult to apply for', particularly where children did not conform to perceptions of disability as a physical problem and who were thus often subject to conflicting decision making. This compounds problems with low take-up. An unpublished report produced in 1998 estimated take up of DLA to be between 30 per cent and 60 per cent.[21] Geographical variations in the award of DLA have also been noted.[22]

Where benefits are awarded then families often experience anxiety about losing them when they are reassessed.[23] 'Downrating' of benefits when they are reassessed can lead to sudden drops in income which are extremely difficult for families to cope with.[24] In addition, if a child receives hospital care for more than 84 days then her/his DLA is reduced.

Some families are caring for more than one disabled child. However, benefits received may not always reflect this[25] and fail to take account of the cumulative effect of having more than one severely disabled child.[26] For example, carer's allowance is paid at a flat rate regardless of the number of people for whom care is being provided.

For those parents who do choose to continue in employment, the childcare element of working tax credit (WTC) is available to assist those on low wages with the costs of childcare. Such support is available to those who work more than 16 hours a week at a level of 70 per cent of the costs up to a maximum of £175 for one child and £200 for two or more children. (This rises to £175 for one child and £300 for two from April 2005, out of which families will be able to claim 80 per cent of the costs from April 2006. However, no account is taken of the extra costs of caring for a disabled child.) Nonetheless, research undertaken by Contact a Family[27] found that using a home care agency with experience of disability issues would cost at least £8 an hour. For a 30-hour week, this would cost £240 and for families with two or more disabled children, the costs would be even more prohibitive. Hence if parents were working full time, and their child required a high level of support, there would be a significant shortfall which they would have to meet from their own resources. When asked what would be most helpful, parents of disabled children participating in the survey indicated that their most favoured option was additional assistance with childcare via tax credits. Nonetheless, it must be acknowledged that the second most favoured option was access to childminders who were trained to care for disabled children and who were prepared to accommodate them. While an increase in financial support would thus be welcomed, there are also issues in relation to the development of additional, appropriately trained, childcare workers.

Additional costs

According to Russell[28] it costs, on average, an additional £99.15 a week (1998 figures) to bring up a disabled child and benefit levels would need to be increased by between £30 and £80 a week (dependent upon age and nature of disability) in order to meet additional costs. Similarly, Dobson and Middleton[29] have calculated that it costs three times more to provide care for a disabled child compared with a non-disabled child. However, determining the extent of additional costs can be difficult as there is often a difference between what families 'actually' spend and what they 'would spend if they had the money to meet these needs'.[30]

Families often report additional costs associated with paying for special foods, additional clothes, heating and laundry, special toys and equipment, transport, hospital visits and appointments, addressing safety issues, paying for childcare and leisure activities. In addition, families often report paying for additional therapeutic input from, for example, occupational and speech and language therapists.[31]

A further additional cost which can be incurred by families of disabled children relates to housing. Nine out of ten families of disabled children in one study reported at least one difficulty with their housing.[32] These problems were not confined to families of children with physical impairments; difficulties with safety within the home and the location of the home were reported as problems for families whose child(ren) had learning disabilities and/or behavioural difficulties. In order to deal with housing problems most families in the study had moved home at least once. One in ten families had received financial assistance to adapt their home and of these, a third had had to make a financial contribution to the costs of adaptation. However, among those who had been assessed as needing to make a financial contribution, one in three had not been able to afford such a contribution and hence the adaptation was not undertaken.[33]

Incurring debts

The combined effect of reduced income and additional expense means that families of disabled children often find it difficult to save and are vulnerable to falling into debt. Seeking to pay off such debts negatively impacts on an already insufficient income.[34] The Social Fund provides one source of additional funding via either loans or community care grants. However, receipt of a loan means that repayments are taken away from already minimal incomes and applications for community care grants are often turned down, with families sometimes unable to appeal within the specified time limits.[35] Families may thus turn to the Family Fund for one-off grants but this is only available until the child is 16.[36]

The effects of poverty

The effects of poverty on disabled children and their families can be both wide ranging and long term. As Emerson[37] notes, the experience of poverty can have a negative impact on the health and well-being of the disabled child, the mother and the family.

Limited income can limit access to activities outside of the home and hence disabled children and their families can become housebound.[38] This means that not only the disabled child and her/his parents become socially excluded but also that siblings can miss out on activities taken for granted by their peers. Social exclusion is thus a major effect of limited income and additional disability related expenditure.

Seeking to cope on a long-term basis on minimal income can lead to family breakdown and have an adverse effect on the health of the parents.[39] Parents report that their own health has suffered due to the worry and stress they experience.[40] When parents become ill, however, their children still require the same levels of support and supervision as normal. If family and friends are unable to offer assistance then support may have to be purchased, further compounding worries concerning finances.

Possible solutions

In the preceding discussion some common areas of difficulty have been identified which both give rise to, and lock disabled children and their families into, living in poverty. It is to be expected then that some common solutions are suggested in the research and the wider literature.

Changes to the benefit system are widely advocated. For example, it is acknowledged that the payment of disability benefits can have a significant and positive impact both on the disabled child and on the wider family hence it is advocated that greater efforts should be placed on increasing take-up of benefits through the provision of better information and advice.[41] It is also suggested that the system for applying for benefits should be simplified such that the award of DLA triggers automatic payment of benefits such as carer's allowance.[42]

In order to further simplify access to benefits, the payment of cash grants at key stages of the child's life (such as at birth, diagnosis, key transition stages such as ages 3, 5, 11 and 16) has been proposed.[43] Preston[44] takes this further and suggests that there should be an automatic annual grant of £500. Payment of such grants would remove the need for repeated applications for additional funds and provide the parents with a degree of flexibility as to how such monies are spent. Similarly it is argued that the use of direct payments (which enable parents to receive funding rather than services hence providing flexibility for parents concerning allocation of such funds) should be encouraged.[45] The extension of council tax discounts and payment of the winter fuel allowance to families of disabled children are also proposed.[46]

Concerns have been expressed in relation to the adequacy of current levels of disability benefits in meeting the true costs of disability[47] and it is suggested that consideration should be given as to whether raising rates of DLA would bring disabled children out of poverty.[48] Allowances for carers are also viewed as requiring change with an increase in carer's allowance being advocated[49] and an additional component being made payable where parents are caring for more than one disabled child.[50]

One difficulty with assessing the adequacy of benefits to meet the true costs of disability, and the numbers of disabled people living in poverty, is the issue of what counts as family income. At present some benefits such as DLA are considered to be income despite the fact that they are meant to cover disability related costs. It is thus suggested that adjustments should be made to the current methods of gathering statistical data concerning poverty such that an adjustment is made for disability and DLA is not regarded as income.[51]

Difficulties with housing have been identified as a problem area for parents of disabled children.[52] Russell[53] thus proposes that the arrangements for payment of the Disabled Facilities Grant should be reviewed.

A final problem with the benefits system is that while funding received has a positive impact on families, such funding can be precarious due to the current system of reviews, downrating and appeals.[54] It is thus suggested that there needs to be better decision making in the process of review[55] and that current arrangements for downrating of benefits while children are in hospital should be re-examined.[56]

Of course some parents will wish to engage in paid employment and hence action is required to support them to remain in, or move into, paid work. The first suggested area for action is to increase the availability of quality childcare facilities which can adequately meet the needs of disabled children.[57] Such targeted childcare should not be focused only on young children since it could also make a positive impact on the lives of disabled teenagers and their families.[58] Furthermore, it is suggested that assistance with childcare costs should be provided for a transitional period prior to taking up employment since this would enable parents to ensure that the arrangements made are suitable and likely to be sustainable.[59] The research undertaken by Contact a Family[60] also suggests that the level of WTC would need to be raised to cover the true costs of childcare for disabled children with complex needs.

The most recent Government proposals for seeking to address the poverty experienced by disabled children and their families are set out in the document *Improving the Life Chances of Disabled People: Final Report*.[61] This report has been published jointly with the Department for Work and Pensions, the Department of Health, the Department of Education and Skills, and the Office of the Deputy Prime Minister. It would thus appear that there is recognition that addressing the problems experienced by disabled children and their families requires joined-up thinking between government departments. The report notes that its recommendations build upon existing policy initiatives relating to children (generally) and disabled children (specifically).

A number of recommendations are made which have relevance to the problems outlined above:

- In principle, individualised budgets should be extended to families of disabled children.
- All 3- to 4-year-old disabled children and children with special educational needs should be able to access the free part-time early education provision and providers should have adequate access to a fully supported early years special needs support coordinator.
- By 2015 all families with a disabled child under 5 should be able to access high-quality, flexible childcare. It is not stated whether this will be at home, in formal settings, or in both.
- Extended schools – which aim to provide 'wrap around' school-based childcare (providing after-hours support) – must be accessible to families with a disabled child over 5.
- The Department for Education and Skills should, with the Family Fund, examine how its remit could be extended to include families with 16- and 17-year-olds.

The individualised budgets are viewed as 'holistically' addressing the families' needs which arise from their child's impairments and it is suggested that they could 'encompass housing, transport, equipment, childcare and support services and take into account the total impact of the child's impairment on family life including siblings and parents'.[62]

It would thus seem that there is an intention to address some of the key issues identified in the research outlined above. Indeed, the provision of individualised budgets would enable families to have a degree of flexibility in managing the funding which is available. However, the extent to which these individualised budgets are made available, and the extent to which they adequately meet needs, remains to be seen.

There are other areas which are not fully addressed within current policy developments, hence they are suggested here as areas still requiring action. There is a need to:

- develop better systems of monitoring the number of disabled children, the number of families with a disabled child and the number of families providing support for more than one disabled child;

- gather further data concerning the actual levels of expenditure incurred by families with disabled children;
- compare this information to the levels of income currently available via the benefits system.

Without such actions the broader issues relating to adequacy of disability and carers' benefits may remain unaddressed and the extent to which the poverty and exclusion experienced by disabled children and their families is reduced may be limited.

Conclusions

As has been seen in this chapter, some actions have already been taken to address the poverty experienced by disabled children and their families and further action is planned. However, not all of the recommendations highlighted in key reports have been addressed. It will thus be necessary both to evaluate the impact of new developments and to press for further action where required, since only by fully addressing the poverty currently experienced by disabled children will they be enabled to escape from the 'roller coaster that is damaging their current lives and jeopardising their future chances'.[63] As Alcock states: 'poverty is not just a state of affairs, it is an *unacceptable* state of affairs – it implicitly contains the question, what are we going to do about it?'[64]

Notes

1 Prime Minister's Strategy Unit, *Improving the Life Chances of Disabled People. Final Report*, Prime Minister's Strategy Unit, 2005

2 G Preston, *Helter Skelter: families, disabled children and the benefit system* (CASE Paper 92), Centre for Analysis of Social Exclusion, 2005

3 Prime Minister's Strategy Unit, *Improving the Life Chances of Disabled People. Final Report*, Prime Minister's Strategy Unit, 2005

4 National Statistics, *Living in Britain: Results from the 2002 General Household Survey*, The Stationery Office, 2004

5 G Preston, *Hard-working Families: caring for two or more disabled children*, Disability Alliance, 2005

6 Prime Minister's Strategy Unit, *Improving the Life Chances of Disabled People. Final Report*, Prime Minister's Strategy Unit, 2005; E Emerson, 'Mothers of children and adolescents with intellectual disability: social and economic situation,

mental health status, and the self assessed social and psychological impact of their child's difficulties', *Journal of Intellectual Disability Research*, 47:4/5, 2003, pp385–99; E Emerson, 'Poverty and children with intellectual disabilities in the world's richer countries', *Journal of Intellectual and Developmental Disability*, 29:4. 2004. pp319–38

7   D Gordon, R Parker, F Loughran and P Heslop, *Disabled Children in Britain: a reanalysis of the OPCS Disability Surveys*, The Stationery Office, 2000

8   N Sharma, *Still Missing Out? Ending poverty and social exclusion: messages to government from families with disabled children*, Barnardo's, 2002

9   E Emerson, 'Mothers of children and adolescents with intellectual disability: social and economic situation, mental health status, and the self assessed social and psychological impact of their child's difficulties', *Journal of Intellectual Disability Research*, 47:4/5, 2003, pp385–99

10 International Council of Nurses, *Nurses: working with the poor against poverty*, International Council of Nurses, 2004

11 DoH, *Valuing People: A new strategy for learning disability for the 21st century*, Department of Health, 2001

12 H Graham and C Power, *Childhood Disadvantage and Adult Health: a lifecourse framework*, Health Development Agency, 2004

13 P Alcock, *Understanding Poverty*, 2nd edition, Palgrave, 1997

14 Ibid.

15 P Kemp, J Bradshaw, P Dornan, N Finch, and E Mayhew, *Routes Out of Poverty*, Joseph Rowntree Foundation, 2004, www.jrf.org.uk (last accessed 14/03/05)

16 G Preston, *Helter Skelter: families, disabled children and the benefit system* (CASE Paper 92), Centre for Analysis of Social Exclusion, 2005; G Preston, *Hard-working families: caring for two or more disabled children*, Disability Alliance, 2005

17 G Preston, *Helter Skelter: families, disabled children and the benefit system* (CASE Paper 92), Centre for Analysis of Social Exclusion, 2005

18 P Russell, *Disabled Children, Their Families and Child Poverty*, Briefing Paper, End Child Poverty and Council for Disabled Children, 2003

19 Ibid.

20 G Preston, *Helter Skelter: families, disabled children and the benefit system* (CASE Paper 92), Centre for Analysis of Social Exclusion, 2005

21 DSS, *First Findings from the Disability Follow-up to the Family Resources Survey*, Research summary 5, Department of Social Services, 1998, unpublished

22 P Russell, *Disabled Children, Their Families and Child Poverty,* Briefing Paper, End Child Poverty and Council for Disabled Children, 2003

23 G Preston, *Hard-working Families: caring for two or more disabled children*, Disability Alliance, 2005

24 G Preston, *Helter Skelter: families, disabled children and the benefit system* (CASE Paper 92), Centre for Analysis of Social Exclusion, 2005

25 G Preston, *Hard-working Families: caring for two or more disabled children*, Disability Alliance, 2005

26 R Tozer and R Shah, *At the Double: supporting families with two or more severely disabled children*, Joseph Rowntree Foundation, 1999

27 Contact a Family, *Childcare Costs for the Parents of Disabled Children*, Contact a Family, 2005

28 P Russell, *Disabled Children, Their Families and Child Poverty*, Briefing Paper, End Child Poverty and Council for Disabled Children, 2003

29 B Dobson and S Middleton, *Paying to Care: the cost of childhood disability*, Joseph Rowntree Foundation, 1998

30 G Preston, *Helter Skelter: families, disabled children and the benefit system* (CASE Paper 92), Centre for Analysis of Social Exclusion, 2005

31 Ibid.

32 B Beresford and C Oldman, *The Housing Needs of Disabled Children: the national evidence*, JRF Findings, 2002, www.jrf.org.uk (last accessed 14/03/05)

33 Ibid.

34 G Preston, *Helter Skelter: families, disabled children and the benefit system* (CASE Paper 92), Centre for Analysis of Social Exclusion, 2005

35 G Preston, *Hard-working Families: caring for two or more disabled children*, Disability Alliance, 2005

36 See Contact a Family and Family Fund, *Debt and Disability: the impact of debt on families with disabled children*, Contact a Family and the Family Fund, 2004

37 E Emerson, 'Poverty and children with intellectual disabilities in the world's richer countries', *Journal of Intellectual and Developmental Disability*, 29:4, 2004, pp319–38

38 G Preston, *Hard-working Families: caring for two or more disabled children*, Disability Alliance, 2005

39 Ibid.

40 G Preston, *Helter Skelter: families, disabled children and the benefit system* (CASE Paper 92), Centre for Analysis of Social Exclusion, 2005

41 Ibid.

42 Ibid.

43 P Russell, *Disabled Children, Their Families and Child Poverty*, Briefing Paper, End Child Poverty and Council for Disabled Children, 2003

44 G Preston, *Hard-working Families: caring for two or more disabled children*, Disability Alliance, 2005

45 P Russell, *Disabled Children, Their Families and Child Poverty*, Briefing Paper, End Child Poverty and Council for Disabled Children, 2003

46 G Preston, *Hard-working Families: caring for two or more disabled children*, Disability Alliance, 2005; P Russell, *Disabled Children, Their Families and Child Poverty*, Briefing Paper, End Child Poverty and Council for Disabled Children, 2003

47 G Preston, *Helter Skelter: families, disabled children and the benefit system* (CASE Paper 92), Centre for Analysis of Social Exclusion, 2005; P Russell, *Disabled Children, Their Families and Child Poverty*, Briefing Paper, End Child Poverty and Council for Disabled Children, 2003

48 P Russell, *Disabled Children, Their Families and Child Poverty*, Briefing Paper, End Child Poverty and Council for Disabled Children, 2003

49 G Preston, *Helter Skelter: families, disabled children and the benefit system* (CASE Paper 92), Centre for Analysis of Social Exclusion, 2005

50 G Preston, *Hard-working Families: caring for two or more disabled children*, Disability Alliance, 2005

51 Ibid.

52 B Beresford and C Oldman, *The Housing Needs of Disabled Children: the national evidence*, JRF Findings, 2002, www.jrf.org.uk (last accessed 14/03/05)

53 P Russell, *Disabled Children, Their Families and Child Poverty*, Briefing Paper, End Child Poverty and Council for Disabled Children, 2003

54 G Preston, *Helter Skelter: families, disabled children and the benefit system* (CASE Paper 92), Centre for Analysis of Social Exclusion, 2005

55 Ibid.

56 G Preston, *Hard-working Families: caring for two or more disabled children*, Disability Alliance, 2005

57 G Preston, *Helter Skelter: families, disabled children and the benefit system* (CASE Paper 92), Centre for Analysis of Social Exclusion, 2005; G Preston, *Hard-working families: caring for two or more disabled children*, Disability Alliance, 2005

58 G Preston, *Hard-working Families: caring for two or more disabled children*, Disability Alliance, 2005

59 Ibid.

60 Contact a Family, *Childcare Costs for the Parents of Disabled Children*, Contact a Family, 2005

61 Prime Minister's Strategy Unit, *Improving the Life Chances of Disabled People. Final Report*, Prime Minister's Strategy Unit, 2005

62 Ibid., p105

63 G Preston, *Helter Skelter: families, disabled children and the benefit system* (CASE Paper 92), Centre for Analysis of Social Exclusion, 2005

64 P Alcock, *Understanding Poverty*, 2nd edition, Palgrave, 1997, p4

Seven

Asylum seeker families

Pamela Fitzpatrick

Introduction

In years to come social historians may regard very favourably some of the Blair Government's bolder policy intentions. However, any achievements on tackling child poverty and institutional racism may well be overshadowed by the Government's increasingly punitive treatment of asylum seeker families.

It is increasingly clear that Government asylum policy directly conflicts with policies on child welfare, social inclusion and anti-discrimination. Over the last decade the law has changed significantly in respect of asylum seekers: they cannot work or claim social security benefits, have no access to permanent housing, and at best receive support that is set well below subsistence level by way of a largely unregulated parallel benefit system.

The difference in treatment of asylum seeker families is highlighted in a recent report.[1] It found that while poverty has been alleviated for some vulnerable groups over the last seven years, asylum policies have led to a reduction in rights for this group in employment, health services, income and housing. According to the report, policies introduced by the Labour Government have helped to make asylum seekers the most socially excluded group in Britain.

Very little thought appears to have been given to the long-term effect of these policies. We should all be concerned for the well-being of asylum seeker families. Those who have been forced to leave their home, who have had to give up their career and leave behind family and friends, will often suffer from severe trauma. Many will also have been tortured and/or imprisoned. It should be obvious that their experience may well affect their ability to care for their children. Apart from the physical scars, they may be depressed, forgetful and withdrawn and find it hard to participate in daily life. Their removal from the benefit system compounds the problem because it forces them into an extremely transient lifestyle which causes difficulty in finding health care or education for their children.

While most asylum seekers are young single men, around 20 per cent of asylum seekers have children. In 2004 33,930 people claimed asylum in the UK.[2] The main countries of origin were Iran, China, Iraq, Somalia, Zimbabwe and the Democratic Republic of Congo.

These figures need to be assessed in the global context. According to the United Nations High Commissioner for Refugees (UNHCR),[3] at the start of 2003 there were approximately 10 million refugees. Of these, 7.5 million were hosted by Asia and Africa. Europe hosted approximately 2.5 million refugees, with Austria, Sweden and Norway receiving the largest numbers of asylum seekers per capita among European countries.

Home Office figures show that at the end of December 2004 a total of 61,625 asylum seekers were receiving support from the National Asylum Support Service (NASS). Of these, 40,750 were supported in NASS accommodation and the remaining 20,875 were receiving subsistence-only support. In addition, it is estimated that local authorities are supporting approximately 7,000 asylum seeking children who have been separated from their parents and have arrived in the UK without any adult carer.

The experience of asylum seekers

The experience of asylum seekers is unique, not only because of their experiences in their homeland and of being forced to leave their home. They are unique in that once they arrive in the UK without any possessions they are forced to live on an income that is far below subsistence level, often for many years. They are vulnerable to destitution, physical assault, sexual harassment, poor health, depression, loneliness, stress and family breakdown.

Children separated from the security of their family, home and country face acute feelings of loss and uprootedness.[4] These children are obviously vulnerable and in need of considerable support. Yet the Audit Commission[5] has identified that despite their great needs, asylum seeker children often do not receive the same standard of care routinely afforded to indigenous children in need, even though their legal rights are identical. Findings by Save the Children[6] and Barnardo's[7] show that their status as asylum seekers is given precedence over their status as children.

Mothers and children

A growing body of research reveals the impact of government policy on asylum seekers. A recent article stated:

> Newborn babies are being taken into care as a result of a government policy that makes their asylum seeking mothers destitute...Under the policy, social workers are being forced to remove children from their families on the basis that they do not have resources to look after them.[8]

Research conducted by Maternity Alliance[9] on asylum seeker mothers revealed that:

- breastfeeding women and their children were going hungry because they did not have sufficient food to eat;
- women who are HIV positive were forced to breastfeed their babies despite the established risk of transmission of the disease, because the Government would not provide them with milk tokens for formula and they did not have any money to buy it themselves;
- accommodation conditions were very poor;
- women were frightened of the risk of their babies catching infections from the filthy shared bathrooms;
- women felt vulnerable to sexual harassment and felt intimidated by single men living in the same accommodation;
- women with young babies had been repeatedly moved around by accommodation providers.

The report also cited information given by the Black Women's Rape Action Project, which estimated that at least half of all women asylum seekers have been raped. One HIV specialist midwife at the project stated that 85 per cent of her caseload of HIV positive pregnant women were asylum seekers.

Unaccompanied asylum seeker children

Many asylum seeker children are not linked with an adult carer who can ensure that their needs are met. Sometimes asylum seeker children will be 'taken in' by members of their community or by extended family members or family friends. Often there is no assessment by social services as to the suitability of the adult to take responsibility for the child[10] – yet this was a major criticism of the authorities involved in the Climbié case.[11]

An asylum seeker child who comes to the attention of the authorities, for example at a port of entry by immigration officials, will be referred to social services. It is not uncommon for social services to refuse to accept that the child is under the age of 18 and to require the child to undergo an x-ray to try to determine her/his age. Such practice is not only harmful to the child but is generally thought not to be an accurate way to assess age.

If the child does get as far as an assessment s/he can be provided with support either under sections 17 or 20 of the Children Act 1989. Section 17 of the Act places a general duty on local authorities to safeguard and promote the welfare of children in their area who are in need by providing a range of services appropriate to those children's needs. The Act defines a child being 'in need' if:

> …he is unlikely to achieve or maintain, or to have the opportunity of achieving and maintaining, a reasonable standard of health or development without the provision for him of services by a Local Authority.

Section 20 of the Act places a duty on authorities to accommodate any child in need in their area where the child appears to require accommodation because her/his parent or carer is unable to provide her/him with suitable accommodation.

Most unaccompanied asylum seeker children should get help under Section 20 of the Act. This would mean that they would usually be placed with foster carers, have an allocated social worker, a care plan and financial support. However, authorities invariably provide support under section 17 rather than section 20 of the Act. The result is that the child is likely to be placed in bed and breakfast accommodation, often outside of the borough in which s/he seeks help, and usually has no further contact with social services. This arises particularly for children who are believed by the authority to be 16 or over, as there appears to be a common belief that there is no power to support children over 16 under section 20. However, the Act makes specific reference to an authority's power to accommodate a child in need who has reached the age of 16. This applies where the authority considers that the welfare of the child would be seriously prejudiced if it does not provide the child with accommodation. This must surely apply in the majority of asylum cases.

Children in detention

A report by Save the Children[12] reveals a catalogue of mental and physical health problems suffered by children currently held in UK detention centres. It accuses the Government of flouting its own guidelines as well as international legislation designed to protect the rights of young people. Among other issues, the report found that women with young babies had only restricted access to nappies and baby milk.

A common complaint among the young children was weight loss, mouth infections and a general failure to thrive. Children who were detained for periods in excess of 100 days suffered from persistent respiratory conditions and skin complaints. In addition to the impact on children's physical health, the report raises concerns about the significant mental health problems. Sleeping and eating difficulties, depression, stress and anxiety were commonplace.

The legal framework

An asylum seeker is someone who has been forced to leave, or who is unable to return, to her/his home country because of a well-founded fear of being persecuted for reasons of race, religion, nationality, membership of a particular social group or political opinion.[13]

Obligations to asylum seekers

The 1951 Refugee Convention, to which the UK is a signatory, obliges the UK authorities to provide refugees with the same treatment, with respect to public relief and assistance, as is accorded to UK nationals.

The UK is also a signatory to the UN Convention on the Rights of the Child. The Convention states that all the rights contained in the Convention apply to all children without exception and that signatory States have an obligation to protect children from any form of discrimination. Article 3 of the Convention states that all actions concerning the child should take full account of her/his best interests. The Convention specifically refers to asylum seeker and refugee children, stating that special protection is to be granted to them.

In addition to these international obligations, asylum seeker children are entitled to most of the protections under the Children Act 1989. Despite these obligations, the Government has legislated to exclude asylum seekers from almost every aspect of welfare support available to the population in general.

Legislative change

The first major changes to the rights of asylum seekers began in 1993.

The Asylum and Immigration (Appeals) Act 1993

The 1993 Act introduced restrictions to social housing for asylum seekers. An asylum seeker would not be accepted as homeless if s/he had any other housing, however temporary, and in any case would only be housed in temporary accommodation while her/his asylum claim was being determined. This process can take years. Asylum seeker families can be kept in poor housing for lengthy periods, with no security, subject to sudden moves and with the consequent difficulties in finding and securing nursery and school places or being able to register with a GP.

Social Security (Persons From Abroad) Miscellaneous Amendment Regulations 1996

In 1996 regulations were introduced to restrict welfare provision to asylum seekers. The regulations removed asylum seekers from entitlement to disability related benefits and family credit. It also removed entitlement to income support (IS), housing benefit and council tax benefit from any person who did not apply for asylum at a port of entry. The effect of the regulations was to leave approximately 70 per cent of asylum seekers without benefit.[14]

The Social Security Advisory Committee (SSAC)[15] was highly critical and recommended that the regulations should not proceed:

> We do not believe that it is acceptable that a solution should be sought by putting at risk of destitution many people who are genuinely seeking refuge in this country, amongst whom may be numbered some of the most vulnerable and defenceless in our society.[16]

The regulations were introduced with only minor alterations and inevitably became subject to a legal challenge. In June 1996 the Court of Appeal held that the rules were both unlawful and inhumane.[17] In striking down the regulations the Court held:

> The regulations contemplate for some a life so destitute that to my mind no civilized nation can tolerate it. I would hold it unlawful to alter the benefit system so drastically as must inevitably not merely prejudice but on occasion defeat the statutory right of asylum seekers to claim refugee status.

The judgment had restored entitlement to benefit for all asylum seekers but this was to be a brief reprieve. Unfortunately, the Court of Appeal had commented that such draconian rules could not be brought in by secondary legislation; they could only be enforceable through primary legislation. The Government, undeterred by the criticisms of the Court, acted promptly to reintroduce the same restrictions by adding them to the Asylum and Immigration Act 1996.

The Asylum and Immigration Act 1996

The Asylum and Immigration Bill received Royal Assent on 24 July 1996, only weeks after the Court of Appeal had struck down the benefit restrictions to asylum seekers. From that date the same benefit restrictions were once again in force.[18] However, the Act went further and allowed for the restriction of child benefit and access to public housing.

The changes led to widespread hardship and homelessness, and many people sought help from their local authority under the National Assistance Act 1948.[19] This Act places a duty on local authorities to accommodate and support a person who is in need of care and attention. Some families were also provided with support under the Children Act 1989. However, there was no consistency among local authorities as to the support provided and many people were refused help.

This led to yet more legal challenges in order to clarify the exact limits of asylum seekers' rights. On 8 October 1996 the High Court[20] held that local authorities had a duty to provide services under the National Assistance Act to any asylum seeker who could show that s/he had no other means of support. These services had to include the bare necessities of life, which included provision for food, shelter and warmth.

By January 1997 over 4,000 asylum seekers were being accommodated by local authorities under either the National Assistance Act or the Children Act, with the numbers set to increase.[21] Perhaps unsurprisingly, local authorities began to complain that they were unable to cope and began to lobby for change.

The Immigration and Asylum Act 1999

The Labour Government came to power in May 1997. It pledged to alleviate the pressure on local authorities and began a review of the system for asylum seekers; in particular, to end the unfair and arbitrary nature of the rules. The result was the Immigration and Asylum Act 1999 which came into force in April 2000. This Act was more draconian than any measures previously introduced by Conservative governments. The intention of the Act was to exclude *all* asylum seekers from access to *all* social security benefits.[22] It introduced the system of dispersal[23] whereby temporary accommodation would be provided to asylum seekers by a new agency, the National Asylum Support Service (NASS), but only on the condition that the asylum seeker moved to a designated dispersal area.

The Act introduced a completely new and separate benefit system for asylum seekers. The benefit levels are much lower than IS levels and the regulations are not subject to the scrutiny of the SSAC.

The Government decided that asylum seekers should largely have a separate currency to other benefit claimants. Therefore, most of their benefit was paid in the form of vouchers rather than cash. The Government also dictated that supermarkets could not give change from the vouchers. Therefore an asylum seeker who purchased an item for £2 and paid with a voucher worth £5 would receive no change; instead, the supermarket concerned was allowed to pocket the excess.

The Act also placed restrictions on asylum seekers accessing support from social services under the National Assistance Act 1948 and sections 17 and 20 of the Children Act 1989.

The Nationality, Immigration and Asylum Act 2002

This Act allows for asylum seeker families to be accommodated in large reception centres. It was also intended that children would be removed from mainstream education and instead educated separately with other asylum seekers. It enables NASS benefit to be withheld from a person who fails to make a claim for asylum as soon as possible after entering the country. This power has led to thousands of people being left homeless and without any means of support. Initially this only applied to single asylum seekers, but the rule has since been extended to families.

Local authorities are prevented by the Act from providing support to failed asylum seekers and to certain European Union (EU) nationals. This excludes those in exactly the same situation as Victoria Climbié (see p102) from accessing support from social services. Consequently, a child such as Victoria would be less likely to come into contact with social services.[24]

Asylum and Immigration (Treatment of Claimants, etc.) Act 2004

The 2004 Act extends the existing power to withhold support from asylum seekers who fail to claim asylum immediately on arrival in the UK to asylum seeker families with children. NASS benefit can be withheld from failed asylum seeker families who refuse to return 'home'. During the passage of the Bill there was much criticism that parents were being forced to leave the UK and return to a place of danger or face having their children removed from them.

The Act allows for the removal of the rule which allowed refugees to receive backdated social security benefit if they had been granted refugee status. Instead, they will have to apply for a repayable loan. This puts the UK in breach of the 1951 Convention on the Status of Refugees and continues the practice of social exclusion of asylum seekers.

Removal of the right to work

A concession that allowed asylum seekers to work if they had been waiting for six months or more for a decision on their asylum claim was withdrawn in 2002.

Restriction of health care

The Government has moved to trying to bring about restrictions in access to healthcare for failed asylum seekers. These measures have been criticised by the Health Select Committee.[25] Under the new rules, treatment with the antiretroviral drugs that can prevent infection with the virus progressing to

AIDS is no longer available to people who have been refused asylum. The Government has justified the restrictions as a necessary measure to prevent health tourists abusing the system. The Committee rejects this on the basis that there was no such evidence. The Committee warns that it is:

> ...deeply concerned that neither the department nor the public health minister appear to have considered or understood the public health implications of refusing HIV treatment to people who, although not legally resident, continue to live in this country.

The returns project

The latest proposal involves the removal of unaccompanied asylum seeker children to Albania. The Government has indicated that no unaccompanied child will be removed from the UK unless there are adequate reception and care arrangements in place in the country to which s/he is to be removed.[26] However, the Government is now indicating that it believes adequate arrangements are in place in Albania.

The power to remove unaccompanied children[27] would appear to conflict with many aspects of the Children Act 1989. An authority can send a child in its care to live outside the UK but this requires the involvement of the family court.[28] A child in voluntary care may only be placed outside the UK with the authority of every person with parental responsibility for that child.[29]

The policy framework

Black and minority ethnic (BME) families are more likely to experience poverty than the population in general.[30] They are more at risk of unemployment, low pay, poor conditions at work and diminished social security rights. However, there is a growing awareness that this poverty does not arise by accident. There is a clear causal effect between racism and poverty. It is evident that poverty among BME families has its routes in past immigration policy. The UK has historically sought to limit entry to the UK, allowing migration only to fill low-paid employment. Entry to the UK has invariably been on condition that there is no access to social security or public housing.

It is ironic that some of the key social policies of this Labour Government have arisen because of the brutal deaths of two black children, Stephen Lawrence and Victoria Climbié. Both deaths led to the setting up of lengthy and expensive inquiries which resulted in extensive policy and legislative changes intended to end institutional racism and protect children. It is questionable whether this has been achieved.

The Macpherson report[31] into the death of Stephen Lawrence identified the existence of institutional racism and warned of the need for public bodies and institutions to examine their policies to ensure that they were not being unwittingly institutionally racist. The report led to the strengthening of existing race relations legislation with the effect that the Government and all public bodies are under a duty to work for the promotion of good race relations.[32]

The Laming Inquiry[33] into the death of Victoria Climbié led to the Government paper *Every Child Matters*[34] which seeks to ensure that children do not fall through the intended safety net of protection for all children. It aims to bring about root-and-branch reform of children's services at every level to ensure that all children and young people can expect:

- to be healthy;
- to stay safe;
- enjoyment and achievement;
- to make a positive contribution;
- to achieve economic well-being.

The Laming Inquiry is particularly pertinent to the current situation of asylum seekers. Victoria Climbié was an 8-year-old girl from the Ivory Coast who came to the UK with her great aunt. She was neglected and tortured and eventually died in horrendous circumstances. In the inquiry into her death Lord Laming stated that there were numerous occasions where those with a legal duty to protect Victoria could have intervened and saved her but they failed to do so.

Victoria was not an asylum seeker; she and her great aunt were French nationals but their immigration status excluded them from claiming benefits and housing under the habitual residence test.[35] To this extent Victoria was in a very similar position to asylum seeker children. Throughout the inquiry parallels were drawn between the position of children such as Victoria who were newly arrived in the UK, and that of asylum seekers.

It is clear from Lord Laming's report that it was the issue of financial support and accommodation that brought Victoria to the attention of social services rather than any child protection issue. Yet the Government subsequently introduced legislation to prevent asylum seekers and EU nationals in the same position as Victoria Climbié from accessing this type of help from social services.[36] Sadly, children who are newly arrived in the UK would appear to be more at risk today as a direct result of this legislation.

Concerns about the apparent tension between child welfare policies and current immigration policy was addressed in a report by the Education and Skills Select Committee.[37] The Committee asked the Minister for Children to respond to the suggestion that immigration policy was fundamentally in contravention of some of the express aims of *Every Child Matters*. The Minister responded:

> ...when we considered this issue in relation to the Children Act, we had to be absolutely clear that the primacy in this issue has to be the immigration control and immigration policy...

The Committee accepted that there were attempts to look after children's welfare within the immigration system, but were concerned that some of the fundamental policy decisions such as the detention of asylum seeking children may make the achievement of the five outcomes outlined in *Every Child Matters* much more difficult for these children.

Poverty, race and entering into care

Poverty and race are key factors in determining whether a child will enter into care. In a study of 2,500 children[38] it was found that, before the children entered care, only a quarter were living with both parents, almost three-quarters of their families were receiving IS, only one in five was living in an owner-occupied household and over half were living in poor neighbourhoods.

The combination of such risk factors was illustrated by comparing the chances of admission into care for two very different types of children. A child aged between 5 and 9, in a two-parent household and whose parents were white owner-occupiers not dependent on social security benefits, had a 1 in 7,000 chance of entering care. A child of mixed race aged between 5 and 9 living in private rented accommodation with a lone parent who received IS had a 1 in 10 chance of entering care.

It would be interesting to apply the same calculation to asylum seeker children. At best, an asylum seeker child can hope to live with parents receiving the equivalent of approximately 70 per cent of the IS level. They are often living in very cramped, dirty and intimidating accommodation or may be homeless, moving around in search of a place to sleep. Many will already have experienced the loss of a parent or other family member and some will witness domestic violence. Now that their parents are denied the right to work they have little hope of lifting themselves out of poverty and the State has largely abdicated responsibility for these children.

The combination of these factors, the past experience of asylum seekers, the high incidence of stress, of physical and mental health problems and marital breakdown, must surely indicate that asylum seeker children are being put at risk of harm or that they risk being separated from their family and entering into care.

Conclusion

The Government considers low income to be a major cause of social exclusion and views work as the best way out of poverty. So why are asylum seekers denied mainstream benefits and prevented from working? The Government says that it is committed to ending child poverty, to stop discrimination and to introduce the concept of human rights. Yet it excludes asylum seekers, adults and children, from all of these provisions.

Why would a government which says that it is committed to social justice embark on such a vicious and sustained attack on the most vulnerable members of our society? Publicly, the policy measures are justified on the basis that it is not an attack on the asylum seekers themselves but a way of preventing them being exploited by ruthless people-traffickers. However, the Government has imposed measures such as the visa system[39] and carriers liability[40] which means that using a people-trafficker is the only way in which an asylum seeker family can enter the UK.

Further justification is given in the guise of being tough in order to prevent 'bogus asylum seekers' coming to claim benefits. Government ministers have repeatedly made statements that asylum seekers come to the UK to claim benefit rather than escape danger, and this has clearly stuck in the public consciousness. Yet the Government's own research into why asylum seekers come to the UK shows that the reasons are nothing to do with claiming support or work.[41] The countries of origin of most asylum seekers are countries which have oppressive regimes or are politically unstable. It is also clear that the West is not bearing the burden of refugees. Figures from the UNHCR show that the UK does not take a disproportionate amount of the world's asylum seekers and of those it takes, only a tiny proportion receive any form of support.

The Government has also sought to justify its approach as a way of preventing the rise of fascism and racism. Adopting Far Right racist policies would seem to many to be a strange way to promote good race relations. A report by the Council of Europe has attributed blame for the increase in racism in the UK to increasingly restrictive asylum and immigration laws.[42] According to the report, the frequent changes to legislation designed to deter people from seeking asylum in the UK have had a central role in the general negative climate concerning asylum seekers and refugees. The report states:

> Many politicians have contributed to, or at least not adequately prevented, public debate taking on an increasingly intolerant line, with at times racist and xenophobic overtones.

In a modern, wealthy state such as the UK it is imperative that social welfare is provided on the basis of need rather than immigration status. To do otherwise perpetuates discrimination and puts children at risk. This was highlighted by Lord Laming, who said:

> The basic requirement that children are kept safe is universal and cuts across cultural boundaries. Every child living in this country is entitled to be given the protection of the law, regardless of his or her background.[43]

Throughout the report Lord Laming makes the point that Victoria Climbié was not viewed as a child but rather through her status in the UK. Had any of the officials charged with her care acted differently she might be alive today. Lord Laming went on to make the point that the only people who actively intervened on Victoria's behalf were those who viewed her firstly as a child. He commented that:

> The success of Ms Ackah and Avril and Priscilla Cameron in identifying the worrying signs that prompted them to seek the intervention of the authorities may have had much to do with the fact that they treated Victoria like any other little girl.[44]

Current government policy is focused on ensuring work for those who can and security for those who cannot. It is about social inclusion and non-discrimination. It targets families in terms of increased benefits and improved health. Yet asylum seekers are not included in this. Asylum policy is about non-integration, about separateness and otherness. Asylum seeker children are not treated as children in the general population and their needs are not determined in the same way as other children. Instead they are viewed first and foremost through their immigration status.

The decision to establish a parallel but third-class financial support system via NASS, initially using vouchers instead of cash, has only served to underline the otherness of the asylum seeker community. The consequences for these children is bleak but the effect of their treatment will no doubt have huge social consequences in the long term.

To ensure that every child in the UK really does matter, it is time for the Government to rethink its stance on immigration and restore the protections of the benefit system, housing and social services to asylum seeker families. To do otherwise is to diminish the findings of Lord Laming and the memory of Victoria Climbié.

Notes

1   J Hills and K Stewart (eds), *A More Equal Society? New Labour, poverty, inequality and exclusion*, Policy Press, 2005

2   National Statistics, *Asylum Statistics: 4th quarter 2004*, United Kingdom, Home Office, 2004

3   UNHCR, *Refugees by Numbers 2003*, United Nations High Commissioner for Refugees, 2003

4   W Ayotte, *Separated Children Coming to Western Europe: why they travel and how they arrive*, Save the Children, 2000

5   Audit Commission, *Another Country – Implementing dispersal under the Immigration and Asylum Act 1999*, Audit Commission, 1 June 2000

6   K Stanley, *Cold Comfort: young separated refugees in England*, Save the Children, 2001

7   R Stone, *Children First and Foremost: meeting the needs of unaccompanied asylum seeking children*, Barnardo's, 2000

8   S Vevers and A Taylor, *Community Care*, 31/3/05–6/4/05, p6

9   J McLeish, *Mothers in Exile: maternity experiences of asylum seekers in England*, Maternity Alliance, 2002

10 K Stanley, *Cold Comfort: young separated refugees in England*, Save the Children, 2001

11 Lord Laming, *The Victoria Climbié Inquiry: Report of an Inquiry*, Cm 5730, HMSO, 2003

12 H Crawley and T Lester, *No Place for a Child – Children in UK immigration detention: impacts, alternatives and safeguards*, Save the Children, 2005

13 UN Convention Relating to the Status of Refugees, 1951

14 Amnesty International, *Slamming the Door: the demolition of the right to asylum in the United Kingdom*, Amnesty International, 1996

15 The SSAC is an independent body which has a statutory function to advise the government on social security regulation changes

16 Report of the Social Security Advisory Committee on The Social Security (Persons from Abroad) Miscellaneous Amendment Regulations 1995, Cm 3062, HMSO, 8 December 1995

17 *R v Secretary of State for Social Security ex parte Joint Council for the Welfare of Immigrants* [1996] 4 All ER 385; *The Times*, 27 June 1996

18 The rules were added in Schedule 1 to the Act

19 See for example, Refugee Council, *Just Existence: a report on the lives of asylum seekers who have lost entitlements to benefits in the UK*, Refugee Council, 1997; M Carter, *Poverty and Prejudice: a preliminary report on the withdrawal of benefit entitlement and the impact of the Asylum and Immigration Bill*, Commission for Racial Equality, 1996

20 *R v LB Hammersmith ex parte M and others*

21 Refugee Council, *Just Existence: a report on the lives of asylum seekers who have lost entitlements to benefits in the UK*, Refugee Council, 1997, p6

22 Some asylum seekers remain eligible for benefit only because they were already in receipt of benefit when the new rules were introduced and therefore receive some transitional protection. Some other asylum seekers are able to receive certain social security benefits because they are able to rely on rights under EC law or various conventions. However, this is a very limited group and entitlement often arises only because of ingenious arguments as to the construction of the law. The clear policy intention is to exclude all asylum seekers from the benefit system.

23 Under the dispersal system, asylum seekers are moved out of London and the South East of England to certain designated areas for asylum seekers

24 section 54 and Schedule 3 of the Nationality, Immigration and Asylum Act 2002

25 House of Commons Health Committee, *New Developments in Sexual Health and HIV/AIDS Policy*, Third Report of Session 2004–05, HC 252-I/HC 252-II, The Stationery Office, 21 March 2005

26 Immigration and Nationality Directorate's Unaccompanied Asylum Returns Programme Policy Framework Document, Home Office, 2 March 2005

27 section 10 Immigration and Asylum Act 1999

28 section 19(1) Schedule 2 Children Act 1989; this relates to children in care under section 31 of the Children Act 1989

29 section 19(2) Schedule 2 Children Act 1989; this relates to children accommodated under section 20 of the Act and to some children receiving help under section 17 of the Act prior to 7 November 2002

30 See Chapter 5 of this book and L Platt, *Parallel Lives? Poverty among ethnic minority groups in Britain*, CPAG, 2002

31 Sir W Macpherson, *The Stephen Lawrence Inquiry: Report of an Inquiry*, Cm 4262-I, The Stationery Office, 1999

32 This follows the amendments introduced by the Race Relations (Amendment) Act 2002

33 Lord Laming, *The Victoria Climbié Inquiry: Report of an Inquiry*, Cm 5730, HMSO, 2003

34 Department for Education and Skills, *Every Child Matters*, Consultation Paper, Cm 5860, The Stationery Office, 2003

35 The habitual residence test was introduced in 1994 as a way of preventing European Union nationals from accessing certain means-tested benefits

36 Schedule 3 Nationality, Immigration and Asylum Act 2002

37 House of Commons Education and Skills Committee, *Every Child Matters*, Ninth Report of Session 2004–05, HC 40-I/HC 40-II, The Stationery Office, 5 April 2005, para 2007

38 A Bebbington and T Miles, 'The background of children who enter local authority care', *British Journal of Social Work*, 19:5, 1989, pp349–68

39 There is currently a list of approximately 80 visa national countries. This means that you must obtain entry clearance abroad before travelling to the UK. The list of visa national states is regularly updated to include any country which might produce asylum seekers.

40 The system of carriers liability imposes fines on airlines or other carriers who bring in asylum seekers to the UK

41 V Robinson and J Segratt, *Understanding the Decision Making of Asylum Seekers*, Home Office Research Study 243, Home Office, 2002

42 The report was produced in 2000 by the Council of Europe's anti-racism body, the European Commission against Racism and Intolerance. It examined prejudice in a number of countries including the UK. CRI(2001)6, *Second report on the UK*, 3 April 2001.

43 Lord Laming, *The Victoria Climbié Inquiry: Report of an Inquiry*, Cm 5730, HMSO, 2003, p346

44 Ibid., p347

Eight
Child poverty in larger families
Jonathan Bradshaw

Background

In 2003/04, while 10 per cent of children lived in a large family (four or more children) they represented 20 per cent of all children living in households with incomes below 60 per cent of the contemporary median before housing costs (BHC). Their poverty rate was 41 per cent BHC and 51 per cent after housing costs (AHC) compared with 16 per cent for children in one-child families BHC and 24 per cent AHC.[1]

We know that large families are more likely to contain younger children, are more likely to belong to a minority ethnic group, have lower levels of employment, be receiving benefits and be social tenants.[2] So large families overlap with high risk groups covered in other chapters in this volume. However, this chapter shows that family size per se is an independent driver of child poverty.

Equity principles would surely demand that a child should not be poor because of the chances of her/his birth order. However, if we had a distributional system entirely determined by the labour market, children in larger families would be more likely to be poor, because earnings are not adjusted by the number of people dependent on them (except to some extent in Japan). It is partly for this reason that welfare states in the industrial world intervene with a package of tax benefits, cash benefits, reductions in charges and direct services which together assist parents with the costs of child rearing. At present our arrangements in Britain do not meet the equity principle that a child should not be poor because of its birth order. What can be done to ensure that policy moves in this direction? If the Government is going to meet its target to eradicate child poverty in a generation, 'work for those who can' and 'welfare for those who cannot' measures need to be extended more successfully than at present to large families.

This chapter will review what we know already about poverty in large families. Then it will present the results of an analysis of the characteristics of large families, explore how policy impacts on large families in Britain, and comparatively, and finally suggest ways in which policy might be developed. The chapter contains some preliminary results of a project on child poverty in large families commissioned by the Joseph Rowntree Foundation, which will be published as a Rowntree Report early in 2006.

What we know already

The association between poverty and family size was the focus of Eleanor Rathbone's *The Disinherited Family*, first published in 1924.[3] It emerged again as one of the studies that led to the rediscovery of poverty – *Large Families in London*.[4] More recently, the Joseph Rowntree Foundation (JRF) commissioned a Ladders out of Poverty (LOOP) review undertaken by Kemp et al.,[5] and they identified large families as having a high risk of poverty. Large families tend to share certain characteristics that are associated with an increased risk of poverty.[6] The LOOP review found that the presence of two or more of these factors in a household heightens the risk of sustained poverty and hardship and we shall explore that further below.

The increased vulnerability of large families to poverty is confirmed by the study carried out by Adelman et al.[7] They found that children experiencing persistent (lasting over three years) and severe poverty (ie, poor on all three poverty measures used by the study) are generally younger, come from large families, from workless households in receipt of benefit, and from households containing at least one adult of non-white ethnicity. Adelman et al.'s analysis of the 1991–99 *British Household Panel Survey* showed that 59 per cent of children who experienced persistent and severe poverty came from a family containing three or more children, while only 24 per cent of children who were classed as 'not poor' belonged to a large family.[8] In a multivariate analysis of the *Families and Children Study* and using a measure of poverty that combines income and lack of necessities, Berthoud et al.[9] found a co-efficient on the poverty risk for large families eight times that of small families.

Willitts and Swales[10] found that the most common reason given by those not working was that they did not want to spend any more time away from their children and this reason was reported most often by large family respondents. The second most important reason for not working for both small and large family respondents was childcare affordability and availability. Besides the costs of childcare, raising a large family also involves extensive co-ordinating arrangements between home, school, childminder, nursery and work.[11] There is evidence to suggest that the provision of part-time statutory pre-school education combined with formal childcare only makes co-ordination arrangements even more complicated.[12] The combination of childcare costs and complex co-ordination arrangements might deter/delay mothers from large families from entering the labour market. Large families are not only more likely to be dependent on out-of-work benefits but they are also dependent on them for longer periods of time.

Child poverty in large families

It is important to be aware of the demographic context. There has been very little reduction in the proportion of women having one or two children over the last 50 years. However, there has been a sharp decrease in the proportions having three and in particular four or more. As a result, the average completed family size is getting smaller and rates of childlessness among women have increased dramatically. Only 9 per cent of the 1945 cohort of women was childless as opposed to 20 per cent of those born in 1965. It is estimated that as many as 25 per cent of the present cohorts of fecund women will remain childless. This has resulted in changes in the composition of family types containing children in Britain. Over the last 30 years there has been a reduction of children living in large (three+ children) families from 43 per cent in 1972 to 32 per cent in 2003.[13]

Figure 8.1 (BHC) and Figure 8.2 (AHC) overleaf show what has been happening to child poverty by the number of children in the family. Overall child poverty rates have been coming down since 1998/99 but both BHC and AHC the child poverty rates in three- and four-child families have been coming down faster than in one- and two-child families. Thus the gap between the child poverty rates (BHC) in one-child and four-child families has diminished from 38 percentage points in 1994/95 to 25 percentage points in 2003/04.

Figure 8.1

Child poverty (% living in households with less than 60 per cent of contemporary median household income) by number of children in the family, BHC

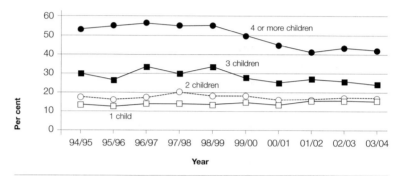

Source: National Statistics, *Households Below Average Income, 1994/5–2003/04*, Department for Work and Pensions, 2005, Table E4.1

Figure 8.2

Child poverty (% living in households with less than 60 per cent of contemporary median household income) by number of children in the family, AHC

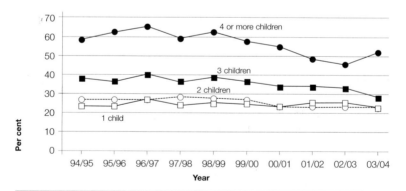

Source: National Statistics, *Households Below Average Income, 1994/5–2003/04*, Department for Work and Pensions, 2005, Table E4.1

As we have learned from the work of Willitts and Swales,[14] large families are different from small families in a number of respects other than family size, and in analysis of the *Family Resources Survey* as part of the JRF project we have taken this further.[15] Large families are more likely to have/be:

• mothers under 24 at first birth;
• a child under 5;
• parents who are not in employment;
• Black, Pakistani or Bangladeshi ethnic origins;
• mothers who left school at 16;
• resident in London or Northern Ireland.

However, many of these characteristics are associated with higher child poverty rates. In order to distinguish between the effects of these factors and family size it is necessary to undertake multivariate analysis. Table 8.1 shows, first the bivariate odds (before controlling for anything else) of a

Table 8.1
Odds of child experiencing poverty

	Not controlling for other factors	Controlling for all other factors
Family size		
1-child family	1.00	1.00
2-child family	1.04***	1.29***
3-child family	1.81***	1.81***
4-child family	3.66***	3.65***
5+-child family	6.56***	3.83***
Family type		
Couple with children	1.00	1.00
Lone parent with children	2.47***	0.33***
Number of earners in household		
Two earners	1.00	1.00
One earner	4.47***	6.02***
No earners	20.51***	48.97***
Mother's age at first birth		
Under 21	1.00	1.00
21 to 27	0.51***	0.83***
28 and over	0.25***	0.66***

	Not controlling for other factors	Controlling for all other factors
Age of youngest child		
4 and under	1.00	1.00
5 to 10	0.98***	1.96***
11 to 15	0.91***	2.48***
16 to 19	0.75***	2.73***
Ethnicity of head of household		
White	1.00	1.00
Mixed	1.04***	1.01 NS
Indian	0.86***	1.13***
Pakistani or Bangladeshi	7.90***	3.68***
Black Caribbean or Black African	1.42***	1.45***
Other	1.89***	1.70***
Mother's age when leaving full-time education		
16 or under	1.00	1.00
Between 16 and 18	0.43***	0.70***
Over 18	0.39***	0.67***
UK region		
London	1.00	1.00
England	0.88***	1.56***
Wales	1.22***	2.25***
Scotland	1.10***	2.00***
Northern Ireland	1.14***	2.36***
Whether there is anyone disabled in the household		
None	1.00	1.00
One or more	0.65***	0.10***

Probability of not being statistically significant: *** = $p<0.001$

NS = not significant

Source: Original analysis of the 2002/3 *Family Resources Survey*: J Bradshaw and E Mayhew, *The Millennium Cohort Survey and Family Resources Survey Analysis*, JRF large families project, Working Paper 4, Social Policy Research Unit, University of York, 2005

child being poor. As suggested above, the odds are higher in large families, in lone-parent families, in workless families, for young mothers, where there is a child aged 4 and under, among certain minority ethnic groups, where mothers left school at 16 and outside England except London. The child poverty rate is lower in a household with a disabled member. This is likely to be because benefits for disabled people are counted as income in the *Family Resources Survey*.

After controlling for all factors simultaneously, family size still remains a strong predictor of child poverty. Indeed, the coefficients on family size only fall for a 5+-child family compared with the bivariate analysis. The coefficients for the other characteristics also change and in the case of some factors, alter direction – eg, age of the youngest child, family type. We have repeated this analysis in the *Millennium Cohort Survey* and family size remains a strong predictor of poverty even after controlling for the similar factors.

Policy

On the face of these results the tax and benefit system does not appear to be very sensitive to the needs of large families.

- Child benefit is paid at a higher rate for the first child in a family and at the same rate for all others. There is no premium as there is in some other countries for large families.
- Working tax credit (WTC) and child tax credit (CTC) are paid at a standard rate for each child.
- The childcare tax credit element only covers a maximum of 70 per cent of childcare costs of up to two children.
- Child support is 17 per cent of earnings for the first child, 20 per cent for the second and 25 per cent for the third and subsequent children.

In examining the treatment of large families by the tax and benefit system, we need to distinguish the package for families with parents in employment and those with parents out of employment.

Parents in employment

It is possible to use the Department for Work and Pensions (DWP) *Abstract of Statistics* to explore how the relative net incomes of families of different sizes at a given earnings level have changed over time. The latest edition of the *Abstract* includes data for each April between 1972 and 2003.[16] In the analysis below we have focused on couples with no children and one, two and three children and selected some years before 1997 and each year since then. For 2004 we have made estimates using

Table 8.2

Net income after housing costs at half average earnings: implied equivalence scales

Year	Implied equivalence scale for a couple with three children (one-child couple = 1.00)
1972	1.36
1982	1.37
1992	1.34
1997	1.35
1998	1.34
1999	1.35
2000	1.35
2001	1.34
2002	1.33
2003	1.33
2004*	1.35

* Estimate assumes £290 a week gross earnings

Source: Department for Work and Pensions, Abstract of Statistics 2004, available at

www.dwp.gov.uk/asd/asd1/abstract/Abstract2004.pdf

the latest DWP *Tax Benefit Model Tables* for April 2004[17] and an estimate of average earnings. Table 8.2 shows the position for families earning half of average earnings, where the net income of families with children is influenced not only by child benefits but also by these in-work benefits: family income supplement, family credit, working families' tax credit, CTC (which is also an out-of-work benefit), WTC, housing benefit and council tax benefit. We have estimated an implied equivalence scale[18] for a couple with three children, with a couple with one child as the base at 1.00. In 1972 a couple with three children received 36 per cent more than a couple with one child on the same earnings. By 1998 that ratio had fallen to 34 per cent more. Since then it has fluctuated and, we estimate, it is now 35 per cent more. So, not much change. However, there has been an improvement in the implied equivalence for families with children over a childless couple – the implied equivalence scale has increased from 1.14 for a one-child family in 1972 to 1.31 in 2004. However, that improvement has been of most benefit to small families.

Out-of-work families

So far we have reviewed the implied equivalence scales in the tax/benefit package for families with children in employment. Now we do the same for families on income support (IS) (or income-based jobseeker's allowance). Again we have used the DWP *Abstract of Statistics* to compare the incomes of families on IS.[19] In this case the series only goes back to 1988 when IS replaced supplementary benefits. Data for 2004 has been estimated from CPAG's *Welfare Benefits and Tax Credits Handbook*. It can be seen in Table 8.3 that since 1988 and especially since 1999 there has been a marked improvement in the implied equivalence scale of couples with children over childless couples. This is because the family premium and child scale rates of IS have both been uprated faster than the adult scale rates. Since 1999 there has also been an improvement in the implied equivalence of a three-child family over a one-child family. This has been achieved as a result of the scale rates for children being uprated more than the family premium in each year since 1999.

Table 8.3

Implied equivalence scales for families on social assistance

Year	Implied equivalence scales (childless couple = 1.00)			Implied equivalence scale for a couple with three children (one-child couple = 1.00)
	1 child	**2 children**	**3 children**	
1988	1.33	1.54	1.75	1.16
1992	1.36	1.58	1.80	1.16
1997	1.36	1.58	1.80	1.16
1998	1.36	1.58	1.80	1.16
1999	1.42	1.67	1.92	1.18
2000	1.50	1.82	2.15	1.22
2001	1.55	1.93	2.31	1.24
2002	1.57	1.97	2.36	1.25
2003	1.63	2.08	2.53	1.28
2004	1.67	2.15	2.64	1.29

Source: Calculated from Department for Work and Pensions, *Abstract of Statistics 2004*, available at www.dwp.gov.uk/asd/asd1/abstract/Abstract2004.pdf

Table 8.4

Comparisons of implied equivalence scales and actual equivalence scales

Scale	Implied equivalence scale for a couple with three children (one-child couple = 1.00)
OECD	1.44
Modified OECD	1.33
McClements BHC*	1.33
Square root of number in household	1.29
Average earnings 2004	1.04
Half average earnings 2004	1.35
Income support 2004	1.29

* Without variations by age

However, this is not to imply that the differentials that now exist between families of different sizes is right or appropriate. The original National Assistance Board scales in 1948 for children were less in comparison to adults than Beveridge had proposed in 1942,[20] and although Beveridge's 1942 proposals were substantially more generous to children than Rowntree's 1935 Human Needs Scale[21] there are still question marks about whether they ever adequately took into account the needs of larger families. In modern times we take account of the relative needs of families of different sizes in research by using equivalence scales, which themselves have very little basis in science.[22] Table 8.4 compares some of the conventionally used equivalence scales with the implied equivalence scales we have derived from net income. The McClements scale currently used in the *Households Below Average Income* series to monitor the anti-poverty strategy (and the modified Organisation for Economic Co-operation and Development (OECD) scale that is going to replace it) are both relatively more generous to large families than the IS implied equivalence. The OECD scale is more generous to large families than all the implied equivalence scales in the tax and benefit system.

However, this only reflects on differentials and again begs the question of adequacy. It is still undoubtedly the case that children in large families have a higher risk of poverty and, if the target to abolish child poverty is to be achieved, policy will need to be geared more towards the needs of large families.

The Government is already aware of the problem of poverty in large families.

- The *Opportunity for All* report[23] acknowledged the problem of poverty in large families and concluded that more research is needed to understand its correlates.
- The House of Commons Work and Pensions Committee's report on *Child Poverty in the UK* has also highlighted the issue of child poverty in large families and suggested that:

  > the national strategy for child poverty should consider including additional financial support for large families, either through a new large family premium in child tax credit, or additional premia for all children.[24]

- The DWP's reply to the Work and Pensions Committee more or less ignored this recommendation.[25]
- However, the *Child Poverty Review* announced 'a long-term aspiration to improve the financial support available to large families'.[26]

'Long-term' implies that it will be achieved by gearing benefit rates towards larger families over a period of years.

In considering policy of this kind, it is important to recognise that in an anti-child poverty strategy there is a trade-off between spending extra money on large families or small families. More children in poverty live in small families, therefore extra cash/tax benefits paid to small families will tend to help more families and lift more children out of poverty – also because small families have smaller gaps between their net income and the poverty threshold. However, as the objective of the anti-poverty strategy is to abolish all child poverty, and given the equity arguments expressed at the start of this chapter, then child poverty in large families needs to be tackled. There are broadly three ways of doing this:

- For families in employment, raise child benefit for large families by paying a premium for the third and subsequent children. A number of countries do this including France, Italy, New Zealand, the Netherlands and Sweden.[27]
- For families with children, increase CTC (and childcare tax credit) for the third and subsequent children.
- For workless families, raise the IS scale rates for the third and subsequent children.

Further work needs to be undertaken to model the most cost-effective mix of these policies. Regard will also need to be had to changes in the structure of incentives between out-of-work and in-work incomes (replacement rates) and also marginal tax rates (the poverty trap). The latter problem should act as a constraint on the extent to which lifting large families out of poverty can be achieved entirely on the basis of means-tested CTC. In order to avoid very high marginal tax rates for large families, some of the extra help will need to be delivered via universal child benefits.

Notes

1 National Statistics, *Households Below Average Income, 1994/5–2003/04*, Department for Work and Pensions, 2005

2 M Willitts and K Swales, *Characteristics of Large Families*, IAD, Social Research Division, Department for Work and Pensions In-house Report, 2003

3 E Rathbone, *Family Allowances: a new edition of The Disinherited Family*, George Allen and Unwin, 1949

4 H Land, *Large Families in London*, Occasional Papers in Social Administration, Bedford Square Press, 1969

5 P Kemp, J Bradshaw, P Dornan, N Finch and E Mayhew, *Routes Out of Poverty: a research review*, Joseph Rowntree Foundation, 2004

6 M Willitts and K Swales, *Characteristics of Large Families*, IAD, Social Research Division, Department for Work and Pensions In-house Report, 2003

7 L Adelman, S Middleton and K Ashworth, *Britain's Poorest Children: severe and persistent poverty and social exclusion*, Save the Children, 2003

8 Ibid.

9 R Berthoud, M Bryan and E Bardasi, *The Dynamics of Deprivation: the relationship between income and material deprivation over time*, DWP Research Report 219, Corporate Document Services, 2004

10 M Willitts and K Swales, *Characteristics of Large Families*, IAD, Social Research Division, Department for Work and Pensions In-house Report, 2003

11 C Skinner, *Running Around in Circles: coordinating childcare, education and work*, Joseph Rowntree Foundation, Policy Press, 2003

12 Ibid.

13 National Statistics, *Social Trends 34*, The Stationery Office, 2004, Table 2.4

14 M Willitts and K Swales, *Characteristics of Large Families*, IAD, Social Research Division, Department for Work and Pensions In-house Report, 2003

15 J Bradshaw and E Mayhew, *The Millennium Cohort Survey and Family Resources Survey Analysis*, JRF large families project, Working Paper 4, Social Policy Research Unit, University of York, 2005

16 Department for Work and Pensions, *Abstract of Statistics 2004*, available at www.dwp.gov.uk/asd/asd1/abstract/Abstract2004.pdf

17 Department for Work and Pensions, *Tax Benefit Model Tables April 2004,* available at www.dwp.gov.uk/asd/asd1/TBMT_2004.pdf

18 Equivalence scales are a means of adjusting income so that it treats different families equivalently. Tax/benefit systems treat families of different types differently so they have implied equivalence scales.

19 Department for Work and Pensions, *Abstract of Statistics 2004*, available at www.dwp.gov.uk/asd/asd1/abstract/Abstract2004.pdf

20 S Baldwin and K Cooke, *How much is enough? A review of supplementary scale rates*, Family Policy Studies Centre, 1984

21 F Field, *What price a child?*, Policy Studies Institute, 1985; J Bradshaw and T Lynes, *Benefit Uprating Policy and Living Standards*, SPRU Social Policy Report 1, University of York, 1995

22 There are also differences in the implied equivalence scales in the different benefit systems for families of different sizes and types which seem to have little to do with independent measures of relative needs (Family Budget Unit: www.york.ac.uk/res/fbu/)

23 DWP, *Opportunity for All, Sixth Annual Report 2004*, Cm 6239, Department for Work and Pensions, 2004

24 House of Commons Work and Pensions Committee, *Child Poverty in the UK: Second Report of Session 2003–04*, Volume 1, The Stationery Office, 2004

25 DWP, *Report on Child Poverty in the UK*, Reply by the Government to the Second Report of the Work and Pensions Select Committee, Session 2003–04 [HC 85-1], Cm 6200, Department for Work and Pensions, 2004

26 HM Treasury, *Child Poverty Review*, The Stationery Office, 2004, p6

27 J Bradshaw and N Finch, *A Comparison of Child Benefit Packages in 22 Countries*, Research Report 174, Department for Work and Pensions, 2002

Nine

Parents in prison: the impact on children

Janet Walker and Peter McCarthy

By 2004, according to the Prison Reform Trust, England and Wales had become the prison capital of Western Europe.[1] At the end of August, the adult prison population stood at 75,183 (70,597 men and 4,586 women).[2] These unprecedented levels of imprisonment have extensive and poorly understood consequences for prisoners' families, especially their children, yet routine information about prisoners' parental status and responsibilities is not collected. These families usually experience stigma and social exclusion within their communities and severe economic hardship which further heightens their sense of loneliness and isolation.[3] The financial cost for families of imprisonment is far more extensive than is commonly recognised[4] and it is hardly surprising that many children feel let down and experience emotional and behavioural problems. Rather than receiving support, however, children are themselves labelled as deviant and excluded even further. In this chapter we explore the extent of the impacts of parental imprisonment, thus reaffirming arguments, based on humanitarianism and the prevention of future offending, that families of prisoners should be better supported and that governments have a responsibility to promote policies which do this.[5]

Forgotten children

We cannot know just how many children experience the imprisonment of a parent, although the Government has estimated in its Green Paper *Every Child Matters*[6] that 4 per cent of children experience the imprisonment of a father during their school years and that every year some 150,000 children experience a parent being put in custody. A national prison survey conducted in 1991[7] found that nearly a third of male prisoners and almost a half of female prisoners were living with dependent children before their sentence. Wellard[8] claimed that around two-thirds of women in prison have at least one child under 18. These are probably underestimates: there are other parents in prison who were not living with their children but still had parental responsibilities before they went into custody; and prisoners, particularly those in gay and lesbian families, may be wary about revealing their parental status for fear that their children might be taken into care.[9]

We have recently completed research which aimed to explore risk, protection and resilience in respect of children with a parent in prison.[10] Questionnaires distributed in eight prisons were completed by 428 fathers and 260 mothers of children aged between 8 and 18. Seventy per cent of the mothers and 60 per cent of the fathers indicated that they had lived with at least one of their children prior to imprisonment. Most (65 per cent) of the mothers and 25 per cent of the fathers were serving their first prison sentence.

Children with a parent in prison are a largely forgotten and vulnerable group who attract little public attention. As Morris noted 40 years ago, every stress suffered by prisoners' families:

> weakens the family and increases the likelihood of other family members, especially the children, becoming social casualties, thus adding not only to the charge upon the community but to the sum of human unhappiness.[11]

Parental imprisonment can cause chaos in children's lives and many children will live in poverty before, during and after imprisonment,[12] yet relatively little is known about the extent of these impacts. Children of prisoners are both silent and silenced within the community.[13] Research has shown, however, that the maintenance of family ties is crucial both to reducing recidivism in prisoners and to preventing their children from getting caught up in a generational cycle of antisocial and offending behaviour.[14] It is likely that children will experience other family changes as a result of the imprisonment of a parent, including changes in living arrangements and a significant reduction in household income,[15] which may also increase their propensity to become involved in criminal activities. The trauma of parental imprisonment has economic, social and emotional dimensions, and Hagan[16] has argued that it can alter the prospects for the family through the:

- strains of economic deprivation;
- loss of parental socialisation through role modelling, support and supervision;

- stigma and shame associated with labelling;
- prevalence of certain types of families, which are more likely to include offenders.

While our primary focus in this chapter is on economic deprivation, it is clear that the other factors both compound and are compounded by low income and poverty.

Family income and deprivation

The imprisonment of a parent usually results in a drop in household income and an increase in outgoings.[17] O'Keefe identified a two-month trough following sentence during which household income is significantly reduced.[18] Many families experience a crisis because benefits and bank accounts are frozen.[19] Although the food bill may be lowered because there is one less mouth to feed, overall expenditure usually increases owing to the need to find money to support the prisoner (phonecards, stamps, stationery, etc.) and to make visits. Since many families experience financial pressures prior to imprisonment, the new burdens merely add to them.

We asked a sample of 48 prisoners (21 women and 27 men) who had maintained contact with their children during their sentence about financial concerns. Fifty-seven per cent of female prisoners and 48 per cent of male prisoners had found it difficult to live on their income before going to prison: 71 per cent of the women and 46 per cent of the men described their income as below average. Although we do not know whether their financial difficulties were associated with their offending behaviour, other research has found evidence of a link between crime and poverty:

> The most powerful drivers of crime are community deprivation and income inequalities resulting from unemployment. Crime is spatially concentrated and associated with homelessness, poor health, parenting factors, drugs and alcohol misuse, school exclusion, leaving care and prison. A criminal record is itself likely to lead to exclusion, having an impact on the chances of obtaining employment in particular.[20]

One father in our study had served seven prison sentences for crimes of burglary. He said he committed crime so that his children would not have to experience the poverty which had blighted his own childhood. He was one of eleven children and had spent eight years in care. He wanted to bring up his children 'to the standards of other people's, wearing good clothes' and to 'keep them out of going to jail'. While he was out of prison his family could live comfortably. When he was in prison, however, the family lost its breadwinner and the loss of income, albeit an illegal one, was felt keenly. This case serves to demonstrate that criminal activities may raise some children out of poverty, and imprisonment may result in families falling back into it. For other families, criminal activities reduce income. One mother we interviewed described how her life was dominated by the need to find £20 a day to feed her drug addiction. Children and young people we talked to described how their mother's addiction had led to hunger, lack of clothing, the selling of furniture, utilities such as gas and electricity being disconnected and, eventually, eviction.

The mother of a 23-year-old woman who had served two prison sentences for shoplifting (to pay for her heroin addiction) tended to give in to her daughter's demands for cash in order to protect her 9-year-old grandson from further upsets, despite her disapproval. She told us:

> If she [the daughter] comes in for £10 – and I know what it is for – rather than have any hassle, I just say to her 'Here you are,' because if I don't she tends to flip. It is not worth the hassle because she will just go and get it off somebody else.

The grandmother and her husband were the full-time carers of their grandson and were finding it extremely difficult to cope because of their own poor health and their daughter's recurrent drug abuse. The grandfather described life as 'a struggle':

> I was earning over £300 a week and...I had a stroke. I am only 53. Lost my job through it and lost my driving licences. I didn't have too much in the bank but what I had has had to help us with everyday outgoings!

The worst aspect of their daughter's release from prison was renewed fear of her stealing from them:

> ... you have spent years getting things you need and then to come in one day and they are not there and you know who has taken them ... I put locks on the doors upstairs.

As a consequence of these stresses, shortly after their daughter's release these grandparents were near breaking point.

This case underlines the differential impacts related to gender. Although 89 per cent of the fathers in our sample indicated that, during their imprisonment, their children were living with and being cared for by the other parent, this was true for only 27 per cent of the mothers. In 43 per cent of the cases in which the mother was in prison the children were looked after by a grandparent, and in 15 per cent they were in the care of other relatives. Some childcare arrangements were particularly complex, with siblings split between family members. One in ten mothers told us that her children were in residential or foster care. This suggests considerably greater disruption in children's lives when mothers go to prison. When fathers go to prison, mothers tend to be left with the burden of coping financially, usually becoming dependent on social security benefits. By contrast, when mothers go to prison the financial burdens may be spread across several households, and grandparents, many of whom may be living on meagre pensions or incapacity benefit, can be especially vulnerable.

One grandmother in our study told us that she learned of the arrest of two of her daughters, who were heroin users, when a social worker knocked on her door at 7am with 11 of her grandchildren in tow. She subsequently took on the full-time care of four of them and arranged for the others to be looked after by other relatives. We know from other research,[21] also, that most grandparents with responsibility for the care of their grandchildren during and after a parent's imprisonment experience financial difficulties. Many give up work or reduce their hours, with adverse impacts on their pension entitlements and savings for retirement. It seems grossly unfair that relatives who provide childcare are not eligible for the childcare element in working tax credit, and we suggest that ways should be found of reimbursing relatives for the costs of additional childcare responsibilities when they look after children in these circumstances.

For the most part, imprisonment brings about a change for the worse in financial circumstances. Although a minority of families find it easier to manage the household finances when a parent goes to prison because money is not being squandered on drugs or alcohol, the majority struggle, and debts may mount. Scarce resources are stretched further as a result of costs associated with supporting and visiting the prisoner. Prisoners frequently ask for money for toiletries and other day-to-day items, and families find it hard to refuse. Prison visits represent another financial drain.

Maintaining family ties

We do not know how many prisoners lose contact with their children, nor how many families split up as a result of imprisonment. It is estimated that about 45 per cent of prisoners lose contact with their families.[22] The strains caused by overcrowding and movement between prisons make maintaining ties difficult. At any one time, 11,000 prisoners are held more than 100 miles from home and over a third of prisons still have no visitors' centre.[23] Many prisons are not family-friendly, despite increasing recognition within the prison service, and by voluntary organisations set up to support prisoners' families, of the importance of maintaining family ties. As the former Director General of the Prison Service stated:

> A stable, supportive family throughout the sentence is a key factor in preventing re-offending on release. I firmly believe that we should do as much as possible to sustain family relationships at what for many will be an especially traumatic time in their lives.[24]

Contact with parents is also important for children, yet a study of young male offenders[25] found that only half of them received visits from their children. This is often the result of poor relationships between parents and the fact that mothers bear the brunt of fathers' imprisonment, socially and economically. Moreover, it is seldom easy for families to visit, especially when the prisoner is located in another part of the country. This is particularly problematic for the children of female prisoners. Although families on benefits such as income support, income-based jobseeker's allowance, tax credit or pension credit can receive financial assistance for visits, the costs can be crippling for those on low incomes just above the qualification bar. Some families in our study found the effort and expense of visits 'horrendous'. One family, for example, had to travel from the south of England to a prison in Northumberland. In another case, a grandmother who was looking after her grandchildren while her daughter was in prison told us:

> We would visit at least once a month. Either myself or my other daughter would take the kids through, but it cost us nearly £100 a time…It is a long day from here. You're going at ten in the morning. By the time you have got lunch, petrol, got them McDonald's on the way home, spending money there, you could get through £100 no problem. And because we work, we don't get compensated.

Many families do not seem to know about the existence of help with travel costs,[26] and others are deterred from claiming because of the perceived bureaucracy. For children there is the added frustration of being unable to interact physically with their imprisoned parent on visits. The Ormiston Children and Families Trust has established special children's visits in a number of prisons,[27] which is an important step forward.

Allowing prisoners access to telephones provides a useful channel of communication: 66 per cent of mothers and 49 per cent of fathers in our study said that they were able to talk to their children at least once a week, although the cost is borne by families. Imaginative projects in some prisons encourage parents to engage with their children by making tapes, writing stories and focusing on the obligations associated with parenthood.[28] More needs to be done, however, if the impacts of these initiatives are to be sustained when prisoners return home. Dennison and Lyon[29] have found that many young offenders do not live up to their good intentions to change for the better, although fathers who maintain family ties while in prison are six times less likely to reoffend[30] if they and their families receive appropriate support on release.

Returning home

Financial and other pressures rarely end when a prisoner is released. A prisoner's return to the family home often places additional pressures on family resources. Some prisoners in our study described themselves as being at 'rock-bottom' when they left prison, particularly as they had little prospect of finding employment. One mother told us:

> I have been looking for work, but I am getting, basically, point blank refused because I've got a criminal record. Even though they've got 'Rehabilitation of Offenders' on the interview form, I'm walking into the interview and they're just saying, 'No... You've got a criminal record. We can't do nowt for you'.

Prisoners are more likely than non-offenders to have received a poor education and to have truanted or been excluded from school and many have never experienced regular employment. Over two-thirds are unemployed at the time they are sentenced,[31] so their chances of finding work on release are minimal. This is arguably more difficult in a climate of increasing intolerance towards anyone who is a known offender. One of the mothers in our sample described how she had spent her sentence (for drug-related offences) reflecting on the harm her addiction was causing her family: her 21-year-old daughter had been evicted when her mother had been sent to prison, and her sons, aged 9 and 12, were living with their grandmother. When we interviewed her towards the end of her sentence, this mother was desperate to make amends on release. She told us:

> I don't want no more of it [prison], I have had enough. And I have seen how upset my kids have been, and how it's disrupted all their lives by us getting made homeless. While I am securely tucked up in jail they are going from hostel to hostel, and it is not fair on them.

When we interviewed her shortly after she had come out of prison, she was managing to keep off drugs despite pressure from dealers in her community. She was certain that the only way to reunite her family was to get a house of her own, but this was proving difficult. Prior to her going to prison, her house had been used by other drug users and disturbances had been reported. As a result, she was evicted and put on the council blacklist. Not only did she now not have a home of her own, but she could not find employment because of her record. She had found a house in the private sector, but could not raise the £500 bond, four weeks' advance rent (£320) and agent's fee:

> It is knocking £1,000. So how am I supposed to find that when I am on income support? What have I got to do … go out and rob to get the deposit?

Sadly, this woman could see no legitimate means of resolving her financial crisis and a return to crime seemed inevitable, despite her desire to be a responsible parent in the future. Social inclusion – the realisation of citizenship economically and socially – militates against crime. Conversely, social exclusion – homelessness, worklessness and social alienation – creates the desperation which frequently gives rise to criminal activities.[32]

Looking to the future

At a seminar held in December 2003 as part of HM Treasury's *Child Poverty Review*, clear evidence was provided about the links between child poverty and families at risk. The risk factors considered included those associated with parental neglect, inconsistent discipline, family disruption and deviant parental behaviours. Children with a parent in prison are likely to experience all these risk factors, which increase poverty of opportunity as well as financial poverty. These children constitute a particularly insecure group, who suffer a range of devastating impacts, and they are more likely than other children to become offenders themselves.[33]

These impacts represent a heightened probability of negative outcomes but do not imply causality. Many high-risk children who have faced extreme stress survive and thrive as stable adults, particularly if they experience positive, supportive relationships and are nurtured through the difficulties and traumas.[34] Some children in our study described the support they had received from their friends and from grandparents which helped them to weather the storms and stay clear of trouble themselves. Nevertheless, the matrix of factors which contribute to low self-esteem and behavioural transgressions are undoubtedly more pronounced when the parents are subjected to repeated arrests and consequently their children experience repeated separation from them.[35] Social exclusion and family disintegration are commonplace,[36] and overwhelming stresses and strains reduce families' abilities to cope with everyday life. Families feel 'guilty by association' and have to deal with stigma and ostracism.[37]

Aungles has argued that partners and parents of prisoners are brought into the penal sphere through 'their hidden labour, their hidden economic subsidies to the state and/or through their hidden punishment'.[38] Little recognition is given to the adjustments family members have to make when a parent goes into and comes out of prison.[39] Children may feel they have to be emotionally brave, giving the impression they are coping, thus losing the support they really need.[40] Some relationships ruptured by imprisonment are never repaired and children may end up being taken into care.[41]

It seems likely that the prison population will continue to rise, placing additional burdens on the benefit system, housing, education, social services and families.[42] Imprisonment can, on occasion, remove parents whose presence is detrimental to family well-being: families of drug abusers frequently describe the relief they feel when the abuser is locked up. Such relief is only temporary, however, as our study has shown. For the most part, imprisonment has extensive negative consequences for families and children, and some 58 per cent of released prisoners return to prison within two years.[43]

Not only is it crucial to find better, less destructive alternatives to custodial sentences, but much more needs to be done to provide appropriate support for families and for parents in prisons in order to assist the maintenance of family ties, ensure adequate housing and protection from poverty during and beyond a parent's imprisonment, enhance parenting skills before parents return to the community, help offenders back into work, and reduce the risk factors for children whose lives are punctuated by the criminal behaviour of their parents. There is an urgent need for more interventions targeted at supporting the children themselves, the indisputably innocent victims of parental imprisonment. Young people with a parent in prison have said that they need someone to talk to, help with visiting, access to information and help with practical issues,[44] but agencies which become involved with prisoners' families often fail to take account of children's specific needs. Schools could undoubtedly do more in this regard.[45] In assessing risk factors for children, there has been a tendency to focus on the parental offending behaviour and to ignore the complex repercussions of imprisonment.

Sending a parent to prison provides a marker for a range of linked effects, all of which contribute to and reinforce the propensity for child poverty. One of the key questions is the extent to which parental criminality constitutes the main risk factor or whether the additional risks associated with the absence of a parent through imprisonment are more pernicious.[46] What is certain is that ways need to be found to reduce those risk factors, promote the protective factors through the maintenance of family relationships and foster resilience. Any help that is available at present tends to be provided by different agencies addressing different problems, with little evidence of joined-up service provision. The voluntary sector has made an important contribution to the rehabilitation and resettlement of offenders for over 100 years, but there has been no clear policy framework, nor an integrated implementation strategy.[47] Both are essential for the well-being of children and for securing the Government's overall vision of eradicating child poverty. Far too many children face stigmatisation, confusion, bullying at school, insecurity, homelessness and poverty as a result of parental imprisonment.

Notes

1   Prison Reform Trust, *England and Wales – Western Europe's Jail Capital*, press release, 2 February 2004, www.prisonreformtrust.org.uk/news-prWeurope's jailcapital.htm

2   Home Office, *Monthly & Quarterly Prison Population Data: England and Wales*, 2004, www.homeoffice.gov.uk/rds/omcsa.html

3   H Codd, 'Prisoners' families: the "forgotten victims"', *Probation Journal*, 45:3, 1998, pp148–54

4   C F Hairston, 'Prisoners and their families: parenting issues during incarceration', in J Travis and M Waul (eds), *Prisoners Once Removed: the impact of incarceration and reentry on children, families and communities*, Washington, The Urban Institute Press, 2003, pp259–82

5   H Codd, Prisoners' *Families and Resettlement: a critical analysis*, European Deviance Group Conference, Preston, April 2005

6   Department for Education and Skills, *Every Child Matters*, Consultation Paper, The Stationery Office, 2003

7   T Dodd and P Hunter, *The National Prison Survey 1991: a report to the Home Office of a study of prisoners in England and Wales carried out by the Social Survey Division of OPCS*, Her Majesty's Stationery Office, 1992

8   S Wellard, 'Prisoners' families', *Family Today*, National Family and Parenting Institute, 2001

9   B Brooks-Gordon, 'Contact in containment', in A Bainham, B Lindley, M Richards and L Trinder (eds), *Children and Their Families*, Hart Publishing, 2003, pp201–334

10 The research is part of an Economic and Social Research Council-funded network, 'Pathways Into and Out of Crime: Risk, Resilience and Diversity'. For information about the network and our research see www.sheffield.ac.uk/pathways-into-and-out-of-crime

11 P Morris, *Prisoners and Their Families*, Allen & Unwin, 1965, p11

12 C Seymour, 'Children with parents in prison: child welfare policy programme and practice issues', *Child Welfare*, 77 (special issue, Children with Parents in Prison), Sept–Oct 1996, pp771–2

13 K Brown, *No-one's Ever Asked Me: young people with a prisoner in the family*, Federation of Prisoners' Families Support Groups, 2001

14 K Laing and P McCarthy, *Risk, Protection and Resilience in the Family Life of Children and Young People with a Parent in Prison: a literature review*, 2005, www.ncl.ac.uk/ncfs/Current%20Research/newcastle_working_paper.pdf

15 K Brown, *No-one's Ever Asked Me: young people with a prisoner in the family*, Federation of Prisoners' Families Support Groups, 2001

16 J Hagan, *The Next Generation: children of prisoners, 2005*, www.doc.state.ok.us/DOCS/OCJRC/ocjrc96/ocjrc19.htm

17 C Noble, *Prisoners' Families: the everyday reality*, Ormiston Children and Families Trust, 1995

18 L O'Keefe, 'The partners of prisoners: their reality, how they contribute to the criminal justice system and prisoner rehabilitation and how we can assist', paper presented at the 'Women in Corrections: Staff and Clients' conference, Australian Institute of Criminology, in conjunction with the Department for Correctional Services SA, Adelaide, 2000, www.aic.gov.au/conferences/womencorrections/okeefe.pdf

19 G Pugh, *Sentenced Families: signs of change for children with a parent in prison*, Ormiston Children and Families Trust, 2004

20 Social Exclusion Unit, *The Drivers of Social Exclusion: a review of the literature for the Breaking the Cycle series*, Office of the Deputy Prime Minister, 2004

21 E Richards, *Second Time Around: a survey of grandparents raising their grandchildren*, Family Rights Group, 2001

22 Department for Education and Skills, *Every Child Matters*, Consultation Paper, The Stationery Office, 2003

23 Fathers Direct, 'A key way to cut criminality is to unlock a man's fatherhood', *Fatherwork*, 2:3, Winter, 2003/04

24 M Narey, *Partners in Prevention: involving prisoners' families in tackling drug misuse*, conference report, ADFAM National and HM Prison Service, 2001

25 G Boswell and P Wedge, *Imprisoned Fathers and Their Children*, Jessica Kingsley Publishers, 2002

26 G Pugh, *Sentenced Families: signs of change for children with a parent in prison*, Ormiston Children and Families Trust, 2004

27 Ibid.

28 Fathers Direct, 'A key way to cut criminality is to unlock a man's fatherhood', *Fatherwork*, 2:3, Winter, 2003/04

29 C Dennison and J Lyon, *Young Offenders, Fatherhood and the Impact of Parenting Training*, Trust for the Study of Adolescence, 2001

30 Prison Reform Trust/Fathers Direct, *Young Fathers: from custody to community*, conference proceedings, 20 February 2003

31 Social Exclusion Unit, *Reducing Reoffending by Ex-prisoners*, Office of the Deputy Prime Minister, 2002

32 J Young and R Matthews, 'New Labour, crime control and social exclusion', in R Matthews and J Young (eds), *The New Politics of Crime and Punishment*, Willan Publishing, 2003

33 Home Office, *Child Poverty and Families At Risk*, seminar, London, 3 December 2003

34 M Ungar, *Nurturing Hidden Resilience in Troubled Youth*, University of Toronto Press, 2004

35 C Seymour, 'Children with parents in prison: child welfare policy programme and practice issues', *Child Welfare*, 77 (special issue, Children with Parents in Prison), Sept–Oct 1996, pp771–2

36 C Gibbs, 'The effect of the imprisonment of women upon their children', *British Journal of Criminology*, 11, 1971, pp113–30; S F Sharp and S T Marcus-Mendoza, 'It's a family affair: incarcerated women and their families', *Women and Criminal Justice*, 12:4, 2001, pp21–49

37 H Codd, 'Prisoners' families: the "forgotten victims"', *Probation Journal*, 45:3, 1998, pp148–54

38 A Aungles, 'Penal policies: the hidden contracts', in P W Easteal and S McKillop (eds), *Women and the Law: proceedings of a conference held 24–26 September 1991*, Canberra: Australian Institute of Criminology, 1993

39 C Noble, *Prisoners' Families: the everyday reality*, Ormiston Children and Families Trust, 1995

40 K Brown, *No-one's Ever Asked Me: young people with a prisoner in the family*, Federation of Prisoners' Families Support Groups, 2001

41 B E Richie, 'Challenges incarcerated women face as they return to their communities: findings from life history interviews', *Crime and Delinquency*, 47:3, 2001, pp368–89

42 J C Travis, E M Cincotta and A L Solomon, *Families Left Behind: the hidden costs of incarceration and reentry*, Urban Institute Justice Policy Centre, 2003

43 N Page, 'What you really need to know about criminal justice', *Rethinking Crime and Punishment*, 2003, www.rethinking.org.uk

44 K Brown, *No-one's Ever Asked Me: young people with a prisoner in the family*, Federation of Prisoners' Families Support Groups, 2001

45 L Dibb (ed), *'I Didn't Think Anyone Could Understand, Miss': Supporting Prisoners' Children in School*, Federation of Prisoners' Families Support Groups, 2001

46 K Laing and P McCarthy, *Risk, Protection and Resilience in the Family Life of Children and Young People with a Parent in Prison: a literature review*, 2005, www.ncl.ac.uk/ncfs/Current%20Research/newcastle_working_paper.pdf

47 CLINKS Prison Community Links, *A Report on Community-based Organisations and Four Prisons in England*, 1999

Ten

Children with disabled parents

Hugh Stickland and Richard Olsen

Introduction

The strong association between child poverty and parental worklessness is well documented. Roughly half of all children in poverty live in a household where no adult is working. At the same time, it is well acknowledged that worklessness is closely associated with disability and poor health. Compared with Britain's overall employment rate of around 75 per cent,[1] the employment rate for disabled people and those with health conditions is roughly 46 per cent[2] (using the Disability Discrimination Act (DDA) definition of disability[3]). It is extraordinary, therefore, given the strength of association between disability, worklessness and child poverty, that the place of disabled parents in debates about child poverty, and in strategies and policies designed to challenge it, has been so weak. This is despite the fact that there are around 1.7 million disabled parents[4] in the UK today, and around 2.2 million children[5] in their care. With 17 per cent of children having at least one disabled parent, it is impossible to ignore the sheer scale of this group of families. Statistics estimate that nearly 700,000 children of disabled parents are living in poverty before housing costs.[6]

This chapter considers poverty among children who have a disabled parent and uses data from a variety of sources to compare the effects on child poverty of parental disability, parental worklessness and family composition. We look at both the composition of those in child poverty, as well as the risk of children in particular sets of circumstances living in poverty. We conclude by arguing that any attempt to reduce child poverty should address poverty among disabled parents.

Policy context

The Government recognises that many disabled people currently receiving incapacity related benefits would like to work, however not all of them are actually able to work, or can find jobs that suit their particular needs. The Department for Work and Pensions' (DWP) *Five Year Strategy*[7] lays out the Government's plans for helping disabled people move into, and stay in, work. At the same time, the Government has a Public Service Agreement (PSA) target to halve child poverty by 2010, on the way to eradicating it by 2020. In addition, the DWP is committed to a number of other PSA targets, which underpin the above goal. These include commitments to:

- reduce the proportion of children living in workless households by 5 per cent between spring 2005 and spring 2008;
- significantly reduce the difference between disabled people's employment rate and the overall employment rate, taking account of the economic cycle, in the three years to March 2008.

As this chapter will show, disabled parents are important to achieving all these goals. However, while the Government has made specific provision for disabled people, and specific provision for parents, there are no goals, targets, interventions or programmes specifically tailored for disabled parents. Indeed, the way in which (lone) parents as one distinct group, and disabled people as another, have been separated in the roll-out of the New Deal is indicative of the way in which parenting and disability have always been constructed as wholly different welfare categories by central government.

Parenting, disability and worklessness

Figure 10.1 opposite shows how the populations of parents, disabled people and workless people in the UK overlap.

The diagram shows that there are approximately 1.7 million disabled parents. This is from a population of 14.1 million parents, and a population of 5.6 million disabled people. Thus, around 12 per cent of all parents are disabled parents, and around 30 per cent of all disabled peo-

Figure 10.1
Disability, worklessness and parenthood

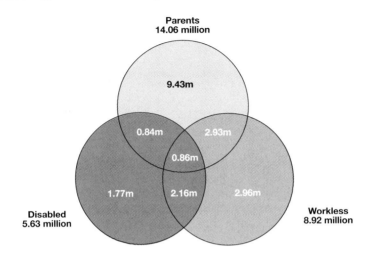

Source: *Labour Force Survey,* National Statistics, Spring 2004,
www.statistics.gov.uk/STATBASE/Source.asp?vlnk=358&More=Y

ple also have children and are thus disabled parents. These figures are
striking similar to figures for the USA. In a 1997 survey, disabled parents
were found to represent 11 per cent of the 57.9 million parents in the USA.
Similarly, the 6.9 million disabled parents in the USA represented around
30 per cent of the approximately 23 million US parents.[8] The diagram also
shows the workless population in Britain. Of the 8.9 million workless people, around a third (just over 3 million) are disabled. Around 3.8 million (42
per cent) are parents.

Having already highlighted the link between paid employment and
poverty, it is worth reviewing the employment rates of disabled parents and
comparing them with other groups such as non-disabled parents.
Employment rates for the key groups are presented in Figure 10.2 overleaf.

The overall UK employment rate stands at 74.7 per cent. This compares with the employment rate for disabled people of 46.3 per cent.
Disabled parents have an employment rate of 49.3 per cent which compares favourably with that of disabled people as a whole. This possibly
reflects the fact that disabled people who are also parents are less likely

Figure 10.2
Employment rates of key groups

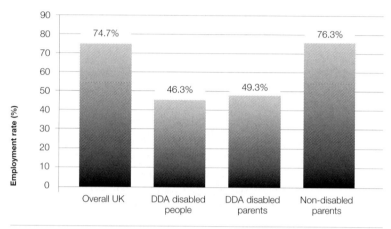

Source: *Labour Force Survey,* National Statistics, Spring 2004,

www.statistics.gov.uk/STATBASE/Source.asp?vlnk=358&More=Y

to be among those disabled people with the most severe impairments who, in turn, are most likely to be out of paid work. However, employment rates for disabled parents are some way behind those of non-disabled parents.

It is helpful, however, to consider disabled parents in terms of the households of which they are a part. The 1.7 million disabled parents live in approximately 1.1 million households. This means that, as one would expect, some disabled parents are married to (or cohabiting with) each other. Figure 10.3 opposite shows employment rates by household. For a household to be considered employed, at least one adult in the household must be in paid employment. Similarly, for it to be disabled, at least one adult in the household must be disabled according to the DDA definitions.

Couples with children where neither are disabled have a household employment rate of over 97 per cent. This drops to 78 per cent when at least one of the couple is disabled. Similarly, for non-disabled lone parents the employment rate of almost 60 per cent is significantly higher than for disabled lone parents at almost 40 per cent. Clearly, then, disability and lone parenthood have significant effects on the likelihood of households having any economically active adult in them.

Figure 10.3
Household employment rates

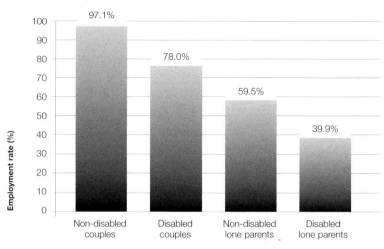

Source: *Labour Force Survey*, National Statistics, Spring 2004,

www.statistics.gov.uk/STATBASE/Source.asp?vlnk=358&More=Y

Disabled parents and child poverty

There are 12.5 million children in Britain today, of which 2.6 million (before housing costs – BHC) and 3.5 million (after housing costs – AHC) are classed as being in poverty. Such figures are based on official definitions of poverty defined by having an income less than 60 per cent of the contemporary equivalised[9] median. Of the 12.5 million children, 2.1 million (17 per cent) have disabled parents. Table 10.1 overleaf shows the composition of the group of children in poverty together with the risk[10] of being in poverty for children with disabled parents.

There is some debate about whether before or after housing costs should carry more weight when discussing poverty, which is applicable to disabled parents also. One could argue that disabled people might experience higher housing costs, due to specific needs or alterations. However, while Table 10.1 shows the risk of poverty increases for children with disabled parents when switching between BHC and AHC, this is mirrored by a similar increase for children of non-disabled parents. When comparing disabled and non-disabled parents, the two measures will give

Table 10.1

Disabled parents and child poverty

	BHC	AHC
No. of children in poverty	2,600,000	3,500,000
No. of children in poverty who have a disabled parent	700,000	800,000
% of all children in poverty living with disabled parents	25%	23%
Total number of children in Britain	12,500,000	12,500,000
Total no. of children with disabled parents	2,100,000	2,100,000
Risk of child poverty for all children with disabled parents	30%	38%
Total no. of children without disabled parents	10,400,000	10,400,000
Risk of child poverty for all children with non-disabled parents	19%	26%

Source: National Statistics, *Households Below Average Income, 1994/5–2003/04*, Department for Work and Pensions, 2005

similar results and therefore the following concentrates on the BHC measure. Measures for the 2010/11 target will also include material deprivation, and analysis will be needed to see whether these pick out any further effects that disability may have.

The composition of overall child poverty on both BHC and AHC measures, shows that roughly one-quarter of children in poverty have disabled parents, and three-quarters have non-disabled parents. However, when considering the risk of child poverty, the importance of disabled parents becomes more apparent. On the BHC measure, 700,000 of the 2.1 million children with disabled parents are in poverty. This means the risk of poverty for children with a disabled parent is 30 per cent. This increases to 38 per cent when using the AHC measure. In comparison, the risk of poverty for children with non-disabled parents is 19 per cent BHC and 26 per cent AHC. Again, these figures demonstrate that the risk of children experiencing poverty is significantly increased when they have at least one disabled parent. However, a cautionary note is required here: the risk of all children experiencing poverty has diminished in recent years, and the risk of the children of disabled parents experiencing poverty has also reduced. The children of disabled parents are still much more likely to experience poverty, but this group has benefited from reductions in overall child poverty.

Poverty by family type

As we have discussed, the Government's measure of child poverty is those children who live in households whose income is 60 per cent or less of the median income. This section uses this measure to consider disabled parents and poverty in more detail.

There is a wealth of data in Table 10.2, which we can break down by the three variables given (working/workless, couple/lone parent and disabled/non-disabled). There is also information on the composition of the 2.6 million children in poverty broken down by these groups, and information on the risk of poverty for children in each of these groups. First, looking at composition, we can break down poverty by the three main groups. Forty-six per cent of children in poverty live in workless households whereas 54 per cent live in working households. Thirty-eight per cent of children in poverty live in lone-parent households, whereas 62 per cent live in couple households. Twenty-seven per cent of children in poverty have at least one disabled parent, whereas 73 per cent do not have a disabled parent.

Looking at workless lone-parent households, the composition shows that the majority of children in poverty have a non-disabled lone parent. We know that roughly 20 per cent of workless lone parents are

Table 10.2

Composition and risk of child poverty by family type (BHC)

Adult disability by family type and economic status		Children in poverty	
		Composition	Risk
workless lone parent	disabled adults	7%	49%
	no disabled adults	22%	51%
workless couple	disabled adults	9%	57%
	no disabled adults	8%	73%
working lone parent	disabled adults	2%	20%
	no disabled adults	7%	14%
working couple	disabled adults	9%	17%
	no disabled adults	36%	12%

Source: National Statistics, *Households Below Average Income, 1994/5–2003/04*, Department for Work and Pensions, 2005

disabled, which is consistent with the figures in the table. The risk of poverty for children in workless lone-parent households is high, but almost equal between disabled and non-disabled lone parents (49 per cent and 51 per cent respectively). This small difference may be due to some disabled lone parents qualifying for incapacity related benefits, which may boost their out-of-work income above that of non-disabled lone parents receiving income support.

The risk of child poverty decreases substantially when a lone parent moves into work and this is reflected by the fact that there are fewer children in poverty in working lone-parent households as compared to workless lone-parent households. Wages and the working tax credit (WTC) raise income levels in lone-parent households, resulting in the risk of poverty falling to 14 per cent for children in non-disabled lone-parent households, and 20 per cent for children in disabled lone-parent households. The effects of disability on employment and poverty will be discussed later, when considering working couples.

Sixty-two per cent of children living in poverty live in couple households. Perhaps unexpectedly, the majority of these (45 per cent) live in households where at least one of the adults is working. The remaining 17 per cent live in workless households.

Of those children living in poverty, who live in a workless couple household, then just over half have at least one disabled parent. However, we know that of all workless couple households with children, two-thirds have at least one disabled parent (see Figure 10.4 opposite).

These figures imply that there is a greater risk for children in workless couple households without disabled parents to be in poverty compared to children in workless couple households with at least one disabled parent. This is confirmed in the risk figures, with 73 per cent of children in non-disabled workless couple households at risk of poverty, compared with 57 per cent where there is at least one disabled parent (see Table 10.2).

Workless couple households where neither parent is disabled are most likely to be claiming jobseeker's allowance (JSA). Workless couple households with at least one disabled parent are likely to be in receipt of an incapacity related benefit. Jobseeker's allowance is designed to be a short-term benefit for those looking for and gaining employment. Couples with children who are dependent on JSA as their main source of income will almost certainly find themselves in poverty. This explains why the risk of poverty for this group is extremely high (with 73 per cent of children in these households in poverty). However, the majority of non-disabled workless couples remain on benefit and are out of work for a short period of time – eg, six months or less (see Table 10.3 opposite).

Figure 10.4

Workless households and disabled parents*

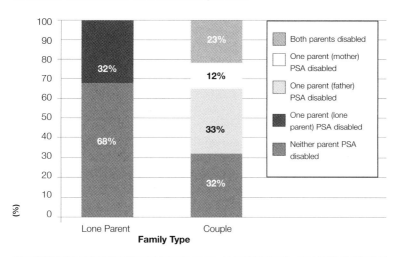

* PSA definition of disabled, which refers to both DDA disabled and those with a work limiting disability

Source: Labour Force Survey, National Statistics, Spring 2003,

www.statistics.gove.uk/STATBASE/Source.asp?vlnk=358&More=y

Table 10.3

Duration of benefit receipt for couples with children by benefit type

	Unemployment benefit	Incapacity related benefit	Others	Total
Under 6 months	18%	5%	2%	25%
6 months to 1 year	6%	4%	1%	11%
1 year to 2 years	5%	7%	1%	13%
2 years plus	3%	44%	4%	51%
Total	32%	60%	8%	

Source: National Statistics, *Client Group Analysis: Quarterly bulletin on families with children on key benefits*,

Department for Work and Pensions, November 2004, www.dwp.gov.uk/asd/cga/asp

Children in poverty in workless couple families where at least one parent is disabled are most likely to be in households dependent on incapacity related benefits. While these benefits are more generous than JSA (typically long-term incapacity benefit (IB) is paid at £76.45 a week, with increases for adult and child dependants, compared with £56.20 a week for JSA, reliance on benefit still means that 57 per cent of children in workless couple households with at least one disabled parent are in poverty. The longer-term nature of these benefits also means that the children may well experience longer, and in some cases much longer, spells of being poor (see Table 10.3).

It should be noted that for both disabled and non-disabled parents who are out of work, additional benefits and payments are available, such as housing benefit, council tax benefit and child tax credit (CTC). Those families who claim these are less likely to be in, or at risk of, poverty.

So, the risk of poverty is lower for children living in workless couple households where there are disabled parents, than where the parents are non-disabled. This is most likely due to differences in the levels at which the different benefits are paid. However, children whose parents are dependent on JSA are likely to be on benefit for shorter durations before moving into employment and often therefore out of poverty. In some senses, there will always be couples with children moving in and out of employment, and thus children who are temporarily in poverty due to the low level of financial assistance available via JSA. In contrast, children in a workless couple household with disabled parents are likely to be dependent on benefit for much longer periods, and some parents may never move into work. Thus although the risk of poverty for this group is lower, the likelihood of being in, or near, poverty lasts for much longer.

Table 10.2 showed that 45 per cent of children in the UK living in poverty live in couple households where at least one adult is working. The majority of these households will have one adult working either at a low wage rate (at or around minimum wage levels) or a limited number of hours, or both. This composition is high because the majority of children in Britain live in working couple households.

The risk of poverty falls dramatically for couples who move from worklessness to employment, from 73 per cent to 12 per cent for non-disabled couples, and from 57 per cent to 17 per cent for disabled couples. However, the risk of poverty is now significantly higher for children with disabled parents than for children with non-disabled parents. This is also true for the children of disabled working lone parents (20 per cent) compared with those of non-disabled working lone parents (14 per cent).

This means that while having a disabled parent in a workless household can insulate children from the likelihood of experiencing poverty (compared to children of non-disabled parents in workless households), having a disabled parent in a household where at least one parent works makes poverty more likely (again compared to being in a non-disabled working household). One reason for this may be the amount and/or type of work open to disabled parents. The likelihood is that disabled parents are more likely to find low-paid and/or part-time work compared to non-disabled parents. This is supported by evidence gathered by the Disability Rights Commission[11] which showed that a third of disabled people aged 18–24 expect to earn less that their non-disabled peers by the age of 30. Furthermore, the employment opportunities of the non-disabled partner of a disabled parent may be affected, particularly if employment has to be combined not only with arranging childcare (as for all families) but also with looking after the disabled parent. These effects on parent and partner employment give non-disabled parents a greater chance of leaving poverty when entering work than disabled parents.

Children whose parents receive wages and tax credits are much less likely to be in poverty than children whose parents receive out-of-work benefits. Take-up of WTC and CTC is relatively high among those families who are eligible. Roughly 4.5 million in-work families are in receipt of WTC and/or CTC. However, the disabled elements of WTC have not been as popular with those who are eligible; just 42,000 in-work families with children are in receipt of the disabled element of WTC. This means that disabled parents moving into work who do not take up the appropriate tax credits may be up to £2,040 a year worse off than if they did.[12]

Additional costs

Of course, in addition to the evidence provided by the data so far, it is important to acknowledge the additional costs involved in being a disabled parent. These may serve further to increase the likelihood of the children of disabled parents experiencing poverty in a way not captured by the discussion so far.

It is likely that some disabled people face higher costs of living in order to maintain a given standard of living that non-disabled people do not face. These higher costs may include extra fuel costs, mobility costs or additional personal care costs which are associated with having a disability but do not yield a higher standard of living compared to the case where there is no disability. Such extra costs will, in some cases, be at least partly mitigated for through additional benefit payments. However, since the additional benefit payments are considered as income and are not discounted for the extra costs of disability, the extent of poverty among the disabled population may be underestimated.[13]

Disabled parents may face additional expenditure in relation to their parenting role. This includes the cost of buying additional specialised equipment, the cost of having to buy more expensive models of ordinary equipment and/or the cost of adapting existing equipment. This additional cost could relate to household appliances such as baby bottle steamers, cots, stairgates and so on, and to the broader paraphernalia of parenting including pushchairs, safety reins, car seats and so on. As an example, a disabled parent may need to rely on several stairgates to prevent access to parts of the house for a young child when other parents would rely on one stairgate and their mobility to ensure safety.

In addition, disabled parents may need to rely on more expensive convenience and/or takeaway food. This may be because their impairments, or lack of support, make preparation of fresh food more difficult. It may also be because they are less easily able to travel between different retailers in order to take advantage of special offers or economies of scale. When they do travel further distances to shop, it is also more likely to involve costly taxi journeys.

Disabled parents may also face additional household running costs. For instance, an inaccessible garden may make it less easy for them to hang washing out in good weather, requiring extra reliance on tumble dryers. Similarly, they may also face extra telephone costs given problems in accessing leisure facilities with their children and the need for often lengthy calls in making travel arrangements or arranging trips.

In summary, then, while the evidence linking parental disability and child poverty is very robust, it would be more so if we were able fully to unpack the additional cost of being a disabled parent. The kinds of additional costs faced by disabled parents will vary depending on circumstances. It is clear, however, that there is at least the potential for additional costs not faced by non-disabled parents and, moreover, not faced by disabled people who are not parents.

Conclusions

The parenting role of disabled adults has attracted increasing attention from policy makers and academics over the last decade or so. This is evident in growing research literature.[14] It is also evident in growing central government concern with disabled parents. This includes the Social Services Inspectorate inspections of services for disabled parents resulting in *A Jigsaw of Services*[15] and in the inclusion of disabled parents in *Fair Access to Care Services* guidance.[16] This is coupled with greater activity in local authorities in particular to recognise this group and to address some of the barriers they face with regard to fulfilling their parenting role. However, the place of parental disability as a key predictor of child poverty has hitherto received little attention.

The data we have presented in this chapter leads us to certain conclusions regarding the impact of parental disability on child poverty. First, children with disabled parents face a significantly higher risk of living in poverty when compared to the children of non-disabled parents. This is true for households with couples and with lone parents. The primary reason for this is the fact that work plays such a significant role in keeping families out of poverty, and that disabled parents are much less likely to be in paid work.

Second, the children of disabled parents in workless families are somewhat less likely to be living in poverty than the children in workless families without disabled parents. The most likely explanation is the higher levels at which IB is paid when compared to JSA. However, although the benefit system is more generous to disabled parents than non-disabled parents, spells of poverty are likely to be much longer for children with disabled parents, given that reliance on IB is generally much more long term than are spells of unemployment for non-disabled parents. The families of disabled parents who are not able to work should receive an income above the poverty line after considering additional costs of parenting and disability, thus ensuring 'security for those who can't work'.

Third, when their parents move into work, the risk of poverty is greater for children with disabled parents than those with non-disabled parents. The most likely cause is the relatively low-paid, part-time and insecure work that disabled people are more likely to take. This discrimination in employment opportunities carries over to non-disabled partners who are more likely to find themselves juggling employment with both parenting and caring responsibilities, jeopardising the levels of income they can attract.

Although disabled parents are key to achieving a number of policy goals and targets, they often fall between the gaps of provision for disabled people and provision for parents. We would argue that for central government initiatives to tackle child poverty to be successful, the poverty experienced by disabled parents has to receive greater attention. This could be done in a number of ways, including reviewing the way in which disability related benefits take into account the additional costs of being a disabled parent, and taking measures to ensure that employment opportunities are fully open to disabled people.

Notes

1 National Statistics, *Labour Force Survey*, Spring 2004, www.statistics.gov.uk/STATBASE/Source.asp?vlnk=358&More=Y – 74.7 per cent
2 Ibid. – 46.3 per cent
3 A person has a disability if s/he has a physical or mental impairment which has a substantial and long-term adverse effect on her/his ability to carry out normal day-to-day activities
4 National Statistics, *Labour Force Survey*, Spring 2004, www.statistics.gov.uk/STATBASE/Source.asp?vlnk=358&More=Y
5 National Statistics, *Households Below Average Income, 1994/5–2003/04*, Department for Work and Pensions, 2005
6 Ibid.
7 DWP, *Department for Work and Penison Five Year Strategy: opportunity and security throughout life*, Department for Work and Pensions, 2005
8 L Toms-Barker and V Maralani, *Challenges and Strategies of Disabled Parents: findings from a national survey of parents with disabilities*, Through the Looking Glass, 1997
9 Equivalised income is income which has undergone a process by which it is adjusted to account for variations in household size and composition. Income is divided by scales which vary according to the number of adults and the number and age of dependants in the household.
10 Risk is the chance of individuals in a group falling below a given threshold. It is calculated as the number in the group below the given threshold divided by the total number in the group.
11 L Sayce, *Disability Rights and Disabled Parents*, Disability Rights Commission, 2004, www.drc-gb.org/publicationsandreports/campaigndetails.asp?section=emp&id=446
12 Inland Revenue, *Child and Working Tax Credits Quarterly Statistics*, National Statistics, December 2004

13 This is a complex area and readers are encouraged to refer to additional work, such as G Preston, *Family Values: disabled parents, extra costs and the benefit system*, Disability Alliance, 2005

14 R Olsen and H Clarke, *Parenting and Disability: disabled parents' experiences of raising children*, Policy Press, 2003; R Olsen and H Tyers, *Think Parent! Supporting disabled adults as parents*, National Family and Parenting Institute/Joseph Rowntree Foundation, 2004; R Olsen and M Wates, *Disabled Parents: examining research assumptions* (Research Review No. 6), Research in Practice, 2003; M Wates, *Disabled Parents: dispelling the myths*, National Childbirth Trust/Radcliffe Medical Press, 1997; M Wates, *Supporting Disabled Adults in their Parenting Role*, Joseph Rowntree Foundation, 2002

15 Department of Health, *A Jigsaw of Services: inspection of services to support disabled adults in their parenting role*, Social Services Inspectorate, 2000

16 See www.dh.gov.uk

Eleven

The social exclusion of Gypsy and Traveller children

Sarah Cemlyn and Colin Clark

Introduction

This chapter examines the poverty and social exclusion of Gypsy and Traveller children in contemporary Britain. We set the scene by exploring who Gypsies and Travellers actually are and how poverty and social exclusion impacts on these minority communities. We examine the legal and policy context and illustrate the ways in which, in particular, Gypsies and Travellers often suffer from spatialised forms of poverty and can be rendered 'invisible' in policy areas where other minority ethnic groups are usually able to at least have their voices heard. We argue that the 'poverty' faced by Gypsy and Traveller children tends to reflect the group's wider relationship with the dominant settled society and the discrimination and denial of human rights they endure across a range of aspects of day-to-day living. To illustrate these points we look at key policy areas and report on how Gypsies and Travellers are provided for in terms of accommodation, education, income/employment, health, family support, and political/community participation.

Who are the Gypsies and Travellers of Britain?

Despite the presence of Gypsy and Traveller groups in Britain for at least 500 years, much confusion surrounds who they are. The terms 'Gypsy' and 'Traveller' (and 'Roma') are not neutral and definitions are heavily contested, both within and outside the communities. We draw on the definitions employed by the Minority Rights Group.[1] These refer to 'Gypsies' as ethnic groups formed by a diaspora of commercial and nomadic groups from India from the tenth century, and subsequent mixing with European and other groups; to 'Travellers' as predominantly indigenous European ethnic groups whose culture is characterised by self-employment, occupational fluidity and nomadism; and to 'Roma' broadly as European Romani-speaking groups.

In Britain there are English Romani Gypsies and Travellers, Welsh Gypsies, Scottish Gypsy-Travellers and Irish Travellers; smaller groups of Roma from Central and Eastern Europe; and 'New' Travellers, now often in their third or fourth generation. Other groups of Travellers also facing discrimination and, potentially, poverty are Travelling Showpeople, Circus Travellers and barge-dwelling Travellers. We use the terms 'Gypsy' and 'Traveller' in this chapter.

How do we define 'poverty' in relation to Gypsies and Travellers?

The definition of poverty employed in this book is highly relevant when examining the situation of Gypsy and Traveller children. Reference to 'participat[ion] in the activities and hav[ing] the living conditions and amenities which are customary…in the societies in which they belong'[2] serves as an apt but also ironic introduction. It is apt because the poverty experienced by some Gypsy and Traveller children involves the deprivation of customary activities (such as attending school), living conditions and basic amenities. It is ironic because to refer to Gypsies and Travellers as 'belonging' to societies is entirely correct but this 'belonging' is heavily debated, with high levels of antagonism and racism expressed publicly, including in the media.

Successive public opinion surveys have shown that these minority groups experience the greatest levels of hostility across many different societies.[3] This hostility interacts with the successive failure of governments to include Gypsies and Travellers in national anti-poverty social exclusion/inclusion agendas, and they also tend to be sidelined in local anti-poverty strategies.[4] However, developments during 2003–04 have witnessed some positive moves including Social Exclusion Unit engagement with 'frequent movers', influential work on site provision by the Institute for Public Policy Research (IPPR),[5] and the Commission for Racial Equality (CRE)[6] targeting anti-Gypsy and Traveller racism and discrimination as urgent priorities in equalities debates.

It is clear that many Gypsy and Traveller children are 'poor' in multiple and different ways. Some are undeniably financially poor, but there are many dimensions to the 'poverty' such groups struggle with. We argue that the dimensions of 'poverty' need to be conceptualised more broadly, in particular regarding spatial poverty. This chapter outlines the extent of knowledge about poverty among Gypsy and Traveller families in the context of their exclusion within economic, social and political systems. Unfortunately, a severe lack of robust quantitative data about aspects of their situation reflects their general exclusion and 'invisibility' within these systems. One disturbing statistic that is often quoted in relation to health is the fact that according to one study only 10 per cent of Gypsies and Travellers in England and Wales are over the age of 40 and less than 1 per cent are over the age of 65.[7] With regard to education, a recent Department for Education and Skills study showed that at least half of all Gypsy and Traveller children in England and Wales drop out of school between Key Stages 1 and 4. The same study also showed very high rates of exclusions.[8]

The legal and policy context

It is important to state that different Gypsy and Traveller groups in Britain are regarded as minority ethnic groups. Both English Romani Gypsies (since 1988) and Irish Travellers (since 2000) are formally recognised as such and have protection under race relations legislation. Scottish Gypsy-Travellers, although accepted by the Scottish Parliament and Executive as an minority ethnic group, have no legal recognition as no test case has yet gone through the courts. Whatever their legal status, a significant aspect of the exclusion endured by Gypsies and Travellers is the *substantive* denial of minority ethnic status and corresponding rights. This takes many forms and operates on a day-to-day basis for many families: they are frequently perceived by service providers, the public and politicians as being social (rather than ethnic) 'drop-outs' or living within 'deviant sub-cultures' that actively reject sedentarist norms.[9]

The pathologisation of Gypsies and Travellers was perhaps most evident in Ireland where Irish Travellers in the 1970s were classified as belonging to a 'sub-culture of poverty'. In these debates Traveller 'sub-culture' was primarily defined in terms of a (negative and 'parasitic') economic relationship with the State, leading to a succession of assimilationist policies that aimed to provide 'solutions' to Travellers' 'problems' and poverty.[10] Such 'solutions' were, of course, resisted by

Travellers and the theory was subsequently refuted by one of its advocates: '[Irish Traveller] culture exists in its own right and is in no way defined by its relationship with the settled society'.[11] However, such popularised notions embed themselves into culture and still influence the thinking of many settled people within Eire and Britain.

Underpinning the continued belief in sub-cultures of poverty within Gypsy and Traveller communities are misunderstandings by settled society of Traveller economies. These economies are largely characterised by family based self-employed activities, and are flexible, adaptable and opportunistic in relation to gaps and opportunities in mainstream economic markets.[12] Similar preferences and patterns of self-employed work operate among New Travellers.[13]

While there has been a decline in traditional work opportunities for some Gypsy and Traveller groups (for example, farm work and scrapping), other new market opportunities are being taken advantage of (for example, car boot sales and market trading). The Gypsy and Traveller economy generates a wide range of economic levels. There are a number of wealthy Gypsies and Travellers who have achieved much success as general traders and in business. Income poverty is not a defining characteristic of Gypsy Traveller culture, although this is not to say it does not exist.

Alongside concerns regarding financial poverty, a *spatial* element to social exclusion is, we would argue, key for many Gypsies and Travellers. This can involve a lack of secure accommodation, safety and access to services. Lack of safety in terms of racist vigilante attacks remains a tragically current issue, as the May 2003 murder of Irish Traveller Johnny Delaney in the Liverpool area illustrates.[14] The social exclusion of Gypsies and Travellers from most settled people's definition and understanding of terms such as 'community'[15] and 'society' is played out through public attitudes and behaviours, and institutional policies and service provision. Gypsies and Travellers are excluded from public space both geographically and culturally[16] and this spatialised poverty is increasingly becoming a central feature of their lives.

What do we know about poverty affecting Gypsy and Traveller children?

Gypsies and Travellers have been rendered 'invisible' in many policy debates and, conversely, highly visible when their physical presence on an unauthorised site upsets the local settled community. Their exclusion as a separately categorised ethnic group from the Census and the ethnic monitoring systems of many public bodies reduces the availability of reliable information about their needs.[17] In schools and colleges there is a more systematic collection of information, although problems and inconsistencies are still evident.[18] Data relating to health has moved on with a recent Department of Health (DoH) study,[19] but a *British Medical Journal* editorial[20] pertinently revealed that there is much more medical research information on the Gypsy *moth* than Gypsy *people*.

The omission of Gypsies and Travellers from mainstream data collection reflects and reinforces a lack of culturally appropriate provision and a failure to include Gypsies and Travellers in policy dialogues and partnerships. The problems faced by community representatives in such partnerships, such as marginalisation, exploitation and discrediting of representative status, are acute for many Gypsies and Travellers.[21] However, their demands to be listened to by government are growing through the work of the Gypsy and Traveller Law Reform Coalition and its constituent groups (a Scottish equivalent started in March 2005).[22]

The 'poverty' faced by Gypsy and Traveller children reflects the group's wider relationship with the dominant settled society and the discrimination and denial of human rights across a range of aspects of day-to-day living. The following sections are organised around key policy areas, including accommodation, education, income/employment, health, family support, and community/political participation. We can only offer a summary account of each in this chapter. Before doing this, however, we need to touch on the universal or specialist services debate.

Clearly, there are advantages as well as disadvantages in mainstreaming and in specialist service provision. On one hand, the mainstreaming equalities agenda has allowed for more collective voices to emerge, it has questioned the pathologisation of Gypsy and Traveller culture within the specialist sector, and has enabled Gypsies and Travellers to claim their right to equality. On the other hand, Gypsy and Traveller items can be pushed to the back of the agenda and their voices drowned out in mainstreaming debates and conferences. We suggest there is a clear place for some specialist provision that bridges the distance between settled services and Gypsies/Travellers and promotes change, access and inclusion in the mainstream – as illustrated by the work of Traveller Education Services (TES) and (scattered) specialist health projects.

Accommodation

Access to secure stopping places has always been an issue for many Gypsy and Traveller families. In England and Wales the 1968 Caravan Sites Act was implemented in a patchy way across the country and local authority inaction and public hostility led to many areas not having any site provision. The Criminal Justice and Public Order Act (CJPOA) 1994 removed the obligation on local authorities to provide sites and led to a severe lack of site accommodation, leaving 25 per cent of the population homeless because they have nowhere legal to park a caravan.[23] Gypsies and Travellers have had to fight through the courts to attempt to get land to locate their trailers. In Scotland there has been no equivalent legislation regarding sites; instead Scottish Gypsy-Travellers have had to rely on 'toleration' policies of local councils.

The effective privatisation of site provision after the CJPOA has led to many families (who could afford to) turning their backs on local authority sites, only to face discrimination in the planning system followed by evictions, courts and hostile newspaper reporting. Examples of such negative reporting appeared during the 2005 election campaign (primarily in *The Sun* and *The Daily Mail*, March and April 2005). However, planning consultation is currently underway[24] but this is accompanied by renewed threats, in the form of Office of the Deputy Prime Minister temporary stop notices,[25] to prevent Gypsies and Travellers from setting up private sites: something they were persuaded to do by the 1990s Conservative Government.

The implications for children of lack of authorised sites are multiple: dangerous and polluting conditions on unauthorised sites; lack of basic services such as water and sanitation; lack of safe play space; and pressure on parents, with resulting health issues.[26] The trauma and psychological effects of eviction are something that many families experience, with threatening and intimidating treatment by bailiffs and police. Repeated eviction leads to lack of access to schools, health and other services.[27] In addition to the heavy personal costs for Gypsies and Travellers, local authorities, police and other agencies have significant financial costs to meet.[28]

On many official sites there are also damaging implications of poor locations (often in areas deemed unfit for housing) and physical conditions. Some are remote from essential services. Unlike housing tenancies, site licence conditions do not give security of tenure, inhibiting local access and inclusion for children and families.[29]

Many Gypsies and Travellers are effectively 'pushed' into housing despite this not being a culturally preferred option.[30] They face similar issues to other population groups: poor conditions; overcrowding, often temporary housing; and also problems of stress because housing is culturally alien, leading to isolation from extended family, racism from neighbours, and worse health than Gypsies and Travellers on sites.[31] These factors produce particular pressures on children.[32]

Education and training

The history of Gypsies' and Travellers' experiences of school has often been negative, from not being admitted or welcomed to facing bullying and a non-inclusive, non-relevant curriculum.[33] There are debates about an assimilationist agenda in the education system[34] that can be perceived and experienced as a cultural threat to Gypsy and Traveller traditions and beliefs.[35] There are continuing parental concerns about potentially damaging influences in secondary school in relation to drugs, sexual mores and sex education classes. However, there is also increasing evidence of Gypsy and Traveller parents wanting school-based education for their children to develop the necessary skills to cope with changing employment patterns.[36]

Equality of access to education and achievement is therefore important to Gypsies' and Travellers' future economic well-being as well as their engagement in political and civic life. However, there are continuing inequalities of access and inclusion,[37] in particular achievement for Gypsy and Traveller children of all ages. They have been seen as the 'group most at risk in the education system'.[38] Contributory factors include racist harassment or bullying and a failure of schools to address it effectively;[39] excessive exclusions from school, sometimes arising out of Travellers' responses to racist incidents;[40] and self-exclusions that may be a response to hostility or other problems.

It does seem that practices in some primary and secondary schools are improving, especially with support from TES, and there are some innovative developments and flexible approaches to post-16 education and vocational training.[41] However, in other schools there is a continuing failure to provide an inclusive environment and an appropriate curriculum in which Gypsy and Traveller children's experience, culture and family based education is validated and built on.[42] In Scotland there is no equivalent to TES.

Income and employment

Although some families are relatively wealthy, both practice knowledge and other studies make clear that some families have few financial resources, despite the paucity of robust data. The Department for Work and Pensions has no separate data on Gypsy and Traveller work patterns or unemployment rates, whereas it does gather such data for most other minority ethnic groups. Although Gypsies and Travellers continue to seek new activities and niche markets, there has been a decline in previous economic outlets, especially in crowed urban environments.[43] Restrictions on travelling and on working activities on official sites have undermined aspects of the Traveller economy.[44] Moreover, many find that simply being a Gypsy or Traveller, and lacking basic literacy skills, will prevent them accessing mainstream wage labour jobs or training. Those who are in waged labour work may face prejudice, hence a preference among some to 'pass' their ethnic identity.

Because of a decline in some former Gypsy and Traveller occupations and lack of opportunity for training and jobs in other areas, access to benefits is important for some families. Again, in this area research has shown levels of discrimination and disadvantage in accessing the benefit system, especially for those who are frequently nomadic.[45] Power[46] has referred to specific surveillance directed towards Gypsies and Travellers on the assumption that they commit fraud. This can result in families being denied benefit where there is little, if any, evidence of actual fraud.

Health

Recent DoH research has found that Gypsies and Travellers had 'significantly poorer health status and significantly more self-reported symptoms of ill-health' than comparators matched for age, gender and economic status.[47] There are clear links between income poverty and poor health across a number of different groups in society, although we argue that poor health in the case of Gypsies and Travellers can also be related to poor service provision. The study found that Travellers were much more likely to experience anxiety and, especially women, depression. Those in houses had significantly higher anxiety levels, something well known anecdotally. A pilot study indicated a detrimental effect on mental health of changes to travelling patterns.[48] Gypsies and Travellers with long-term illness were more likely to be on a council site or in a house, and those who rarely travelled had the worst health status, though causality cannot be determined here. Almost all the Gypsy and Traveller interviewees had lived a travelling lifestyle at some stage and many hoped they or their children and grandchildren would return to it.[49]

Most prior studies have been localised area or practitioner studies related to maternal and child health.[50] These indicated higher morbidity levels for Gypsies and Travellers than the rest of the population.[51] The DoH study found no significant reported differences with pregnancy or childbirth, but the report of *The Confidential Enquiries into Maternal Deaths* found that Travellers have 'possibly the highest maternal death rate among all ethnic groups' associated with substandard care.[52] Smaller studies have found higher infant mortality and perinatal death rates, higher levels of children's infectious diseases and of child accident rates.[53]

Despite clearly indicated patterns of health needs, Gypsies and Travellers have numerous problems accessing health care, particularly registering with a GP.[54] The DoH study explored barriers including communication difficulties, lack of trust, and lack of cultural competence among medical and reception/front-line staff.[55] However, specialist health visitors were highly rated and have facilitated access, as informal studies have illustrated.[56] Overall, many Gypsy and Traveller children are denied rights to basic conditions for healthy development and may miss out on effective health care.

Family support and social work

Gypsy and Traveller culture is strongly family orientated and child-centred. For many it is strong family and extended family networks that offer support in times of trouble. There are limited numbers of research studies examining the relationship between social work and Gypsies and Travellers,[57] and imprecise information about the nature and levels of contact because of lack of monitoring. Parry et al.[58] concluded that Gypsies and Travellers had more contact with social workers than some other service-providing professionals, but other studies have indicated distance between them.[59] What is identifiable is that practice with Gypsy and Traveller children and families is variable in quality and frequently fails to acknowledge cultural issues, especially of housed Travellers, while 'race' equality policies often ignore them altogether.[60] Vulnerable Gypsy and Traveller children may be ignored because they do not fit mainstream systems,[61] and there is little promotion of culturally relevant services such as fostering. The most vulnerable Gypsy and Traveller children may then be further marginalised and isolated.

Sensitive outreach with Gypsy and Traveller communities in non-crisis situations, or at a minimum, partnership with more knowledgeable organisations, could promote better communication and facilitate the kind of holistic approach to family support and child protection that is required by government policy. There are a handful of specialist approaches that can build contact and better mutual understanding[62] but these rare posts are vulnerable to cuts.

Community and political participation

The one positive aspect to emerge in the last decade has been Gypsy and Traveller organisations engaging with more direct and sustained political activism. The Gypsy and Traveller Law Reform Coalition has brought together different organisations under a collective banner of campaigning for formal and substantive civil rights.[63] The Coalition has attracted key partnerships with outside agencies, such as the IPPR and the CRE, and has had a significant role in shifting government thinking on planning, accommodation and broader social policy concerns. For this work the Coalition won the 2004 Liberty Human Rights Award.

Prior to the Coalition, smaller groups like the Gypsy Council worked hard to get Gypsy and Traveller issues on the political agenda. The Coalition brings the advantages of shared resources and a stronger collective 'voice', challenging the traditional exclusion from civic and political engagement. Young people are also involved in activism and making their 'voices' heard.[64] Some of the most passionate activists are young women.

Conclusion

Overall, what are the key policy and service delivery lessons? Secure and appropriate accommodation remains central. We suggest that active and energetic consultation with Gypsies and Travellers across key service areas is a priority. Serious thinking is needed on the 'visibility' of the Gypsy and Traveller presence in public policy vis-à-vis data collection methods in relevant research projects and scoping exercises. Gypsies and Travellers should be included in ethnic monitoring systems, and in 'race' equality strategies. At the service level, training to promote more culturally sensitive responses, more accessible forms of communication, and outreach either directly or in partnership with more specialist services, have all been advocated. This is particularly true in relation to access to better information and advice regarding training and employment courses as well as social security services. The central message we hope to convey is that progress in the areas of accommodation, education, health, and 'race' equality will generate improvements in the way that Gypsy and Traveller children experience family life in Britain and minimise their chances of slipping into poverty and being socially excluded.

Notes

1   J P Liégeois and N Gheorghe, *Roma/Gypsies: a European minority*, Minority Rights Group, 1995, p6

2   'Individuals, families and groups in the population can be said to be in poverty when they lack the resources to obtain the types of diet, participate in the activities and have the living conditions and amenities which are customary, or are at least widely encouraged and approved, in the societies in which they belong' (P Townsend, *Poverty in the United Kingdom: a survey of household resources and standards of living*, Penguin, 1979, p31)

3   I Hancock, 'Duty and beauty, possession and truth: lexical impoverishment as control', in T Acton and G Mundy (eds), *Romani Culture and Gypsy Identity*, University of Hertfordshire Press, 1997, pp180–87; Stonewall, *Profiles of Prejudice: the nature of prejudice in England*, Stonewall/Citizenship 21 Project, 2003

4   Social Exclusion Unit, *Minority Ethnic Issues in Social Exclusion and Neighbourhood Renewal*, Cabinet Office, 2000

5   H Crawley, *Moving Forward: the provision of accommodation for Travellers and Gypsies*, Institute for Public Policy Research, 2004

6   CRE, *Gypsies and Travellers. A Strategy for the CRE 2004–2007*, Commission for Racial Equality, 2004

7   Judicial Studies Board, *Equal Treatment Bench Book, Equality Before Courts and Tribunals*, 2004, section 1.5.8, Roma and Travellers, www.jsboard.co.uk/etac/etbb/benchbook/et_01/et_mf08.htm#158

8   DfES, *Ethnicity and Education: the evidence on minority ethnic pupils,* January 2005, Department for Education and Skills, 2005, www.standards.dfes.gov.uk/ethnicminorities/links_and_publications/EandE_RTP01_05/

9   R McVeigh, 'Theorising sedentarism: the roots of anti-nomadism', in T Acton (ed), *Gypsy Politics and Traveller Identity*, University of Hertfordshire Press, 1997, pp7–25

10 M Collins, 'The sub-culture of poverty: a response to McCarthy', in M McCann, S O Siochain and J Ruane (eds), *Irish Travellers: culture and ethnicity*, Institute

of Irish Studies, 1994, pp130–133; Dublin Traveller Education and Development Group, *Reach Out: report by the DTEDG on the Poverty 3 Programme 1990–1994*, Pavee Point Publications, 1994

11 P McCarthy, 'The sub-culture of poverty reconsidered', in M McCann, S O Siochain and J Ruane (eds), *Irish Travellers: culture and ethnicity*, Institute of Irish Studies, 1994, p128

12 C Clark, '"Not just lucky white heather and clothes pegs": putting European Gypsy and Traveller economic niches in context', in S Fenton and H Bradley (eds), *Ethnicity and Economy: race and class revisited*, Palgrave, 2002; J Okely, *The Traveller Gypsies*, Cambridge University Press, 1983

13 L Webster and J Millar, *Making a Living: social security, social exclusion and New Travellers*, Joseph Rowntree Foundation/Policy Press, 2001

14 Kirby Times, 'Justice for Johnny Delaney', 2003, www.kirkbytimes.co.uk/news_items/2003_news/justice_for_johnny_delaney.html

15 J Brent, 'Community without unity', in P Hoggett (ed.), *Contested Communities: experiences, struggles and policies*, Policy Press, 1997

16 D Sibley, *Outsiders in Urban Society*, Palgrave, 1981; A Bancroft, '"No interest in land": legal and spatial enclosure of Gypsy-Travellers in Britain', *Space and Polity*, 4:1, May 2000

17 R Morris, 'The invisibility of Gypsies and other Travellers', *Journal of Social Welfare Law*, 21:4, 1999, pp397–404; P Niner, *The Provision and Condition of Local Authority Gypsy/Traveller Sites in England*, Office of the Deputy Prime Minister, 2002

18 K Bhopal, J Gundara, C Jones and C Owen, *Working Towards Inclusive Education: aspects of good practice for Gypsy Traveller children*, DfEE Research Report No 238, Department for Education and Employment, 2000

19 G Parry, P Van Cleemput, J Peters, J Moore, S Walters, K Thomas and C Cooper, *The Health Status of Gypsies and Travellers in England*, Report of Department of Health Inequalities in Health Research Initiative Project 121/7500, University of Sheffield, 2004

20 M McKee, 'The health of Gypsies', *British Medical Journal*, 315, 1997, pp1172–3

21 S Cemlyn, *Policy and Provision by Social Services for Traveller children and families: report of research study*, University of Bristol, 1998

22 Gypsy and Traveller Law Reform Coalition, 2005, www.travellerslaw.org.uk/

23 CRE, *Gypsies and Travellers: a Strategy for the CRE 2004–2007*, Commission for Racial Equality, 2004; D Hawes and B Perez, *The Gypsy and the State: the ethnic cleansing of British society*, 2nd edition, Policy Press, 1996

24 ODPM, *Planning for Gypsy and Traveller Sites*, Office of the Deputy Prime Minister, 2004, www.odpm.gov.uk/stellent/groups/odpm_planning/documents/page/odpm_plan_033598.pdf

25 ODPM, *Temporary stop notices*, Office of the Deputy Prime Minister, 2004, www.planningportal.gov.uk/england/government/en/1110214696189.html

26 Chartered Institute of Environmental Health, *Travellers and Gypsies: an alternative strategy*, CIEH, 1995; L Hughes, *My Dream Site*, Children's Society, Children's Participation Project, 1998

27 D Kenrick and C Clark, *Moving On: the Gypsies and Travellers of Britain*, University of Hertfordshire Press, 1999; M Hyman, *Sites for Travellers*, London Race and Housing Research Unit, 1989; R Morris and L Clements (eds), *Gaining Ground: law reform for Gypsies and Travellers*, University of Hertfordshire Press, 1999

28 R Morris and L Clements, *At What Cost? The economics of Gypsy and Traveller encampments*, Policy Press, 2002

29 CRE, *Gypsies and Travellers: a Strategy for the CRE 2004–2007*, Commission for Racial Equality, 2004

30 G Parry, P Van Cleemput, J Peters, J Moore, S Walters, K Thomas and C Cooper, *The Health Status of Gypsies and Travellers in England*, Report of Department of Health Inequalities in Health Research Initiative Project 121/7500, University of Sheffield, 2004; P A Thomas and S Campbell, *Housing Gypsies*, Cardiff Law School, 1992

31 G Parry, P Van Cleemput, J Peters, J Moore, S Walters, K Thomas and C Cooper, *The Health Status of Gypsies and Travellers in England*, Report of Department of Health Inequalities in Health Research Initiative Project 121/7500, University of Sheffield, 2004

32 S Cemlyn, 'Assimilation, control, mediation or advocacy? Social work dilemmas in providing anti-oppressive services for Traveller children and families', *Child and Family Social Work*, 5:4, 2000, pp327–41; D Morran, 'Negotiating marginalized identities: social workers and settled Travelling People in Scotland', *International Social Work*, 45:3, 2002, pp337–51; R Morris and L Clements, *Disability, Social Care, Health and Travelling People*, Traveller Law Research Unit, 2001

33 C Clark, 'The United Kingdom: England, Northern Ireland, Scotland and Wales', in Save the Children Fund, *Denied a Future? The right to education of Roma/Gypsy and Traveller children*, Save the Children Fund, 2001, pp206–301; S Lee, 'Shirley Lee … telling her own story', in P Saunders, J Clarke, S Kendall, A Lee, S Lee and F Matthews (eds), *Gypsies and Travellers in their own words*, Leeds Traveller Education Service, 2000, pp138–46; B Plowden, *The Plowden Report: children and their primary schools*, Her Majesty's Stationery Office, 1967; Department of Education and Science, *Education for all* (the Swann Report), Her Majesty's Stationery Ofice, 1985

34 C Clark, ' "Educational Space" in the European Union: social exclusion or assim-

ilation of Gypsy/Traveller children?', *Social Work in Europe*, 4:3, 1997, pp27–33; B Jordan, 'From interdependence to dependence and independence: home and school learning for Traveller children', *Childhood*, 8:1, 2001, pp57–74; D Mayall, *English Gypsies and State Policies*, University of Hertfordshire Press, 1995; J Okely, 'Non-territorial culture as the rationale for the assimilation of Gypsy children', *Childhood*, 4, 1997, pp63–80

35 C Derrington and S Kendall, *Gypsy Traveller Students in Secondary Schools: culture, identity and achievement*, Trentham Books, 2004; C O'Hanlon and P Holmes, *The Education of Gypsy and Traveller Children: towards inclusion and educational achievement*, Trentham Books, 2004

36 K Bhopal, 'Gypsy Travellers and Education: changing needs and changing perceptions', *British Journal of Educational Studies*, 52:1, 2001, pp47–64; B Jordan, 'From interdependence to dependence and independence: home and school learning for Traveller children', *Childhood*, 8:1, 2001, pp57–74

37 Save the Children Fund, *Denied a Future? The right to education of Roma/Gypsy and Traveller children*, Save the Children Fund, 2001

38 DfES, *Aiming High: raising the achievement of Gypsy Traveller pupils*, Department for Education and Skills, 2003

39 C Derrington and S Kendall, *Gypsy Traveller Students in Secondary Schools: culture, identity and achievement*, Trentham Books, 2004; E Jordan, 'Exclusion of Travellers in state schools', *Educational Research*, 43:2, 2001, pp117–32; G Lloyd and J Stead, '"The boys and girls not calling me names and the teachers to believe me": name calling and the experiences of Travellers in school', *Children and Society*, 2001, pp361–74

40 Ofsted, *The Education of Traveller Children*, Office for Standards in Education, 1996; C Power, *Room to Roam: England's Irish Travellers*, Action Group for Irish Youth/Community Fund, 2004

41 C Clark, 'The United Kingdom: England, Northern Ireland, Scotland and Wales', in Save the Children Fund, *Denied a Future? The right to education of Roma/Gypsy and Traveller children*, Save the Children Fund, 2001, pp206-301; C Clark, 'It is possible to have an education and be a Traveller: education, higher education and Gypsy-Travellers in Britain', in I Law, D Phillips and L Turney (eds), *Institutional Racism in Higher Education*, Trentham Books, 2004; C O'Hanlon and P Holmes, *The Education of Gypsy and Traveller Children: towards inclusion and educational achievement*, Trentham Books, 2004

42 C Kiddle, *Traveller Children: a voice for themselves*, Jessica Kingsley Publishers, 1999; Save the Children Fund, *Denied a Future? The right to education of Roma/Gypsy and Traveller children*, Save the Children Fund, 2001

43 C Power, *Room to Roam: England's Irish Travellers*, Action Group for Irish Youth/Community Fund, 2004

44 C Kiddle, *Traveller Children: a voice for themselves*, Jessica Kingsley Publishers, 1999

45 C Clark, 'Race, ethnicity and social security: the experience of Gypsies and Travellers in Britain', *Journal of Social Security Law*, 6:4, 1999, pp186–202; L Webster and J Millar, *Making a Living: social security, social exclusion and New Travellers*, Joseph Rowntree Foundation/Policy Press, 2001

46 C Power, *Room to Roam: England's Irish Travellers*, Action Group for Irish Youth/Community Fund, 2004, p7

47 G Parry, P Van Cleemput, J Peters, J Moore, S Walters, K Thomas and C Cooper, *The Health Status of Gypsies and Travellers in England*, Summary of Report to the Department of Health, University of Sheffield, 2004, p5

48 P Van Cleemput and G Parry, 'Health status of Gypsy Travellers', *Journal of Public Health Medicine*, 23:2, 2001, pp129–34

49 G Parry, P Van Cleemput, J Peters, J Moore, S Walters, K Thomas and C Cooper, *The Health Status of Gypsies and Travellers in England*, Report of Department of Health Inequalities in Health Research Initiative Project 121/7500, University of Sheffield, 2004

50 For example E Anderson, 'Health concerns and needs of Travellers', *Health Visitor*, 70, April, 1997, pp148–50; H Beach, *Injury Rates in Gypsy-Traveller Children*, MSc in Community Child Health Dissertation, University of Wales College of Medicine, 1999; J Pahl and M Vaile, *Health and health care among Travellers*, University of Kent, 1986

51 E Anderson, 'Health concerns and needs of Travellers', *Health Visitor*, 70, April, 1997, pp148–50; J Pahl and M Vaile, *Health and Health Care among Travellers*, University of Kent, 1986; P Van Cleemput, 'The health care needs of Travellers', *Archives of Disease in Childhood*, 82:1, 2000, pp32–7

52 G Lewis and J Drife, *Why Mothers Die, 1997–1999: the Confidential Enquiries into Maternal Deaths in the United Kingdom*, RCOG Press, 2001, p41

53 H Beach, *Injury Rates in Gypsy-Traveller Children*, MSc in Community Child Health Dissertation, University of Wales College of Medicine, 1999; G Feder, *Traveller Gypsies and Primary Health Care in East London*, PhD thesis, St Thomas's Hospital Medical School, University of London, 1994; S Hajioff and M McKee, 'The health of the Roma People: a review of the published literature', *Journal of Epidemiology and Community Health*, 54, 2000, pp864–69; M Hennick, P Cooper and R Diamond, *Primary Health Care Needs of Travelling People in Wessex*, University of Southampton, 1993; R Morris and L Clements, *Disability, Social Care, Health and Travelling People*, Traveller Law Research Unit, 2001; J Pahl and M Vaile, *Health and Health Care among Travellers*, University of Kent, 1986

54 G Feder, 'Traveller Gypsies and primary care', *Journal of the Royal College of*

General Practitioners, 39, 1989, pp425–29; G Parry, P Van Cleemput, J Peters, J Moore, S Walters, K Thomas and C Cooper, *The Health Status of Gypsies and Travellers in England*, Report of Department of Health Inequalities in Health Research Initiative Project 121/7500, University of Sheffield, 2004; D Hawes, *Gypsies, Travellers and the Health Service*, Policy Press, 1997

55 P Van Cleemput, K Thomas, G Parry, J Peters, J Moore and C Cooper, *The Health Status of Gypsies and Travellers in England: Report of Qualitative Findings*, University of Sheffield, 2004

56 S Cemlyn, 'Traveller children and the State: welfare or neglect?', *Child Abuse Review*, 4, 1995, pp278–90; R Morris and L Clements (eds), *Gaining Ground: law reform for Gypsies and Travellers*, University of Hertfordshire Press, 1999; R Morris and L Clements, *Disability, Social Care, Health and Travelling People*, Traveller Law Research Unit, 2001

57 J Butler, *Gypsies and the Personal Social Services*, Social Work monographs, University of East Anglia, 1983; S Cemlyn, *Policy and Provision by Social Services for Traveller Children and Families: report of research study*, University of Bristol, 1998; D Morran, 'Negotiating marginalized identities: social workers and settled Travelling People in Scotland', *International Social Work*, 45:3, 2002, pp337–51

58 G Parry, P Van Cleemput, J Peters, J Moore, S Walters, K Thomas and C Cooper, *The Health Status of Gypsies and Travellers in England*, Report of Department of Health Inequalities in Health Research Initiative Project 121/7500, University of Sheffield, 2004

59 J Butler, *Gypsies and the Personal Social Services*, Social Work monographs, University of East Anglia, 1983; S Cemlyn, 'From Neglect to Partnership? Challenges for social services in promoting the welfare of Traveller children', *Child Abuse Review*, 9, 2000, pp349–63

60 D Morran, 'Negotiating marginalized identities: social workers and settled Travelling People in Scotland', *International Social Work*, 45:3, 2002, pp337–51

61 C Power, *Room to Roam: England's Irish Travellers*, Action Group for Irish Youth/Community Fund, 2004

62 S Cemlyn, 'From neglect to partnership? Challenges for social services in promoting the welfare of Traveller children', *Child Abuse Review*, 9, 2000, pp349–63; C Power, *Room to Roam: England's Irish Travellers*, Action Group for Irish Youth/Community Fund, 2004

63 Gypsy and Traveller Law Reform Coalition, 2005, www.travellerslaw.org.uk/

64 S Cemlyn, 'Groupwork as a tool in the celebration, resourcing and development of Gypsy and Traveller culture', in T Mistry and A Brown (eds), *Race and Groupwork*, Whiting and Birch, 1997, pp110–37; C Kiddle, *Traveller Children: a voice for themselves*, Jessica Kingsley Publishers, 1999

Twelve

Young people leaving care: poverty across the life course
Mike Stein

Introduction

Young people leaving care are one of the most disadvantaged groups of young people in society. Not only have many experienced abuse, neglect, or difficulties at home, but coming into care has often failed to compensate many of these young people, so by the time they leave – often at a far younger age than other young people leave home – their life chances are very poor. Research has shown that many are likely to face multiple disadvantages including poverty. This is a consequence of their pre-care, in-care, leaving care and after-care 'life course' experiences including:

- their poor family backgrounds and damaging intra-family experiences, including abuse and neglect;
- the failure of care to provide stability and compensate young people in care;
- low levels of educational attainment and post-16 participation;
- leaving care at a younger age than other young people leave home;
- being a young householder, moving often and experiencing homelessness;
- being a young parent.

For the year ending March 2003, 8,307 young people aged 16–18 and over left care in the UK; a majority of these (4,722) at just 16 and 17, defined as a 'child' under the UN Convention on the Rights of the Child but nevertheless having to cope with adult responsibilities.[1] Just under 3,585 left at 18 – although in England between March 2000 and 2003 there has been an increase, from 42 per cent to 51 per cent, of those leaving at 18 and over.[2]

This chapter will review the research evidence and performance data in respect of the three main pathways taken by these young people: from school into post-16 education, employment and training; from living in care to moving into accommodation; and from leaving care and becoming a parent. It will be argued that during these transitions, the risk of poverty and social exclusion of care leavers is greater in comparison to many other young people; but these transitions, as well as the implications for policy, need to be considered in the wider context of their life course.

Care leavers' pathways

Education, employment and training

Analysis of the *Youth Cohort Study* shows that there is a clear association between post-16 educational achievement and the pathway to well-paid, more secure employment. Conversely, young people who leave school at 16 are at greater risk of poverty.[3]

Research carried out in England, Scotland and Northern Ireland shows that young people leaving care have lower levels of educational attainment at 16 and 18 and lower post-16 participation rates than young people in the general population.[4]

The 1998 National Priorities target in England (Performance Assessment Framework CF/A2), was that at least three-quarters of young people leaving care aged 16 or over should have one or more GCSEs/GNVQs by 2002–03.[5] Table 12.1 overleaf sets out the UK figures for the years 2002 and 2003.

Government performance data for England indicates a slow but steady improvement, in that that the percentage of care leavers with at least one qualification (one GCSE or GNVQ pass at any grade) has risen steadily from 31 per cent in 1999–2000 to 44 per cent in 2002–03. However, where comparable data is available in 2002–03, the 44 per cent for looked-after young people contrasts sharply with 95 per cent for all Year 11 young people. Not only that, it is disturbing that even if the Government's 75 per cent target was met, young people leaving care would still have significantly lower outcomes than other young people.

Recent figures for England indicate some progress in that 53 per cent of looked-after children in Year 11 achieved at least one GCSE at

Table 12.1

Proportion of children leaving care aged 16 or over with one or more GCSEs/GNVQs[a] in 2002 and 2003

Country	2002	2003
England	41%	44%
Wales	30%	39%
Scotland	42%	42%
Northern Ireland	44%	42%

[a] At least one qualification at SCQF level 3 in Scotland

Sources: Department for Education and Skills, *Statistics of Education: outcome indicators for looked after children, Twelve months to 30 September 2003, England*, 2004; National Assembly for Wales, *Children Looked After by Local Authorities, 31 March 2003*, 2004, www.lgdu-wales.gov.uk/eng/ pss.asp?cat= 201&year=2003; Scottish Executive, *Children's Social Work Statistics 2002–03*, 2004, www.scotland.gov.uk/ stats/bulletins/00287-00.asp; E Mooney, P McDowell and K Taggart, *Northern Ireland Care Leavers (2002/03)*, 2004, www.dhsspsni.gov.uk/publications/2004/NI-CareLeavers-A4Pub.pdf

grade A* to G or a GNVQ and 37 per cent of this group achieved five or more GCSEs or equivalent at these grades.[6]

Also, when comparisons are made for A*–C grades, in 2001–02, just 8 per cent of young people in Year 11 in England who had spent at least one year in care gained five or more GCSEs, compared with half of all young people. In the same year almost half had no qualifications at GCSE level. Of Year 11 pupils who had been in care for one year or more, 42 per cent did not sit GCSEs or GNVQs, compared to just 4 per cent of all children.[7]

Research carried out in England, Scotland and Northern Ireland shows that care leavers are less likely to be engaged in post-16 education, employment and training than other young people aged 16–19 in the population, having between 2 and 2.5 times the unemployment rate for young people in the same age group.[8]

However, compared to earlier research, two recent studies suggest an increase in the proportion of young people participating in post-16 education. Broad's research, carried out before and after the implementation of the Children (Leaving Care) Act 2000, shows an increase from 17.5 per cent in 1998 to 31 per cent in 2003. This includes a very small percentage, estimated at around 1 per cent, who entered higher education.[9] In the second study, carried out after the Act, just over a third of young people (35 per cent) were participating in post-16 education.[10]

Official data (Performance Indicator CF/A4) from England for 2001–02 shows that 46 per cent of care leavers (with whom local authorities were in touch) at age 19 were in education, employment or training compared with 86 per cent of all young people aged 19 in the population as a whole.[11] Data for 2003, for England, Wales, Scotland and Northern Ireland, indicates that 49 per cent, 48 per cent, 40 per cent and 44 per cent respectively of care leavers were in education, employment and training.[12]

The high proportion of young people not engaged in education, employment and training, as well as the low-paid employment of many others, results in many young people struggling on relatively low incomes. In a recent study of care leavers, the modal income for the sample (n=106) was at the benefits level (£42.70), as many as 95 per cent had received financial help under section 23 of the Children (Leaving Care) Act 2000 or section 24 of the Children Act 1989, and just under a third were finding it very difficult to manage.[13]

Leaving care, housing and homelessness

Families provide a lot of assistance for young people during their journey to adulthood. Living at home, returning home at times of difficulty, as well as financial, practical and emotional support may all protect young people from poverty.[14]

Many care leavers who move into their own accommodation are faced with renting a room and managing their accommodation at just 16 and 17, on a very low income.[15] They are more likely than those of similar age to move regularly and be over-represented among the young homeless population. Comparative research drawing on data from England and Northern Ireland showed that 15 per cent of young people in England and 20 per cent in Northern Ireland experienced homelessness at some point within six months after leaving care.[16]

In a 2001 Scottish survey 61 per cent of care leavers had moved three or more times, and 40 per cent reported having been homeless since leaving care.[17] Research comparing homeless with non-homeless young people found that those who were homeless were 10 times more likely to have been in care during childhood and that between a quarter and a third of rough sleepers were once in care.[18]

For the year ending March 2003, 93 per cent of care leavers in England, and 91 per cent in Wales, were in accommodation deemed 'suitable'. The Scottish Executive identifies 20 per cent of young people as experiencing homelessness in the year after leaving care, 10 per cent moving more than three times and 40 per cent remaining in the same accommodation.[19]

Leaving care and parenthood

Teenage motherhood is associated with a high risk of poverty through reduced employment opportunities, dependency on benefits, social housing, as well as poorer physical and mental health.[20]

Research carried out in England, Scotland and Northern Ireland shows that young women care leavers, aged 16–19, were more likely to be a young parent than other women of their age group.[21] Both having young children (if the youngest child is under 5) and being a young mother (under 25) is also associated with poverty.[22]

A study of inter-generational transmission of social exclusion estimates that young people who have been in care are two and a half times more likely to become adolescent parents than other young people,[23] and data from the British cohort study indicates that children of women who have spent time in care themselves are two and a half times more likely to go into care than their peers.[24]

Young parenthood, under certain conditions, may also be beneficial. There is evidence from young mothers who had been in care of a feeling of maturity. The gains for some included reduced isolation, a renewal of family links, and improved relationships with their mothers and their partners' families.[25] However, a qualitative study of young mothers who had been in care found that they faced a range of problems including financial difficulties, problems in relation to accessing services and coping with parenthood as well as in leaving care.[26]

Poverty among care leavers: a life course perspective

For many young people leaving care the three pathways to adult citizenship, discussed above, are often pathways to poverty.[27] However, these pathways need to be considered as part of their life course, as it is often as a consequence of their pre-care, in-care, and leaving care experiences that many are likely to have multiple disadvantages that predispose them to poor life chances, including poverty and social exclusion.

First, the disadvantaged social class position of families from which many young people enter care and the associated cultural barriers will have a major influence upon their low educational achievement, especially for those young people who enter care during their school years.[28]

Second, most of these young people will have experienced damaging intra-family relations that may have included neglect and poor parenting, or physical, emotional or sexual abuse, experiences that are likely to impact upon their emotional and intellectual development.[29]

Third, against this background, the purpose of care should be to compensate these young people. The foundation stone is stability. However, a consistent finding from research studies of young people leaving care, carried out between 1980 and 2004, has been their experience of instability and placement disruption following their initial or later separation from their birth families. In these studies between 30 and 40 per cent of young people had four plus moves, and within this group between 6 and 10 per cent had a very large number of moves, as many as 10 or more.[30]

The failure to compensate these young people may well contribute to the multiple disadvantages many care leavers experience. In addition to the poor career, householder and parental pathways discussed above, care leavers are more likely than other young people to have poor mental health, drug and alcohol problems, and to be involved in offending, than their peers. These disadvantages make it difficult for young people to secure and sustain employment, thus also contributing to their likelihood of being poor.[31]

Fourth, as discussed in the introduction to this chapter, many of these young people will experience accelerated and compressed transitions to adulthood. A consistent finding from studies of care leavers is that a majority move to independent living at just 16 or 17, whereas most of their peers remain at home well into their twenties, and for many of these young people, leaving care is a final event – there is no option to return in times of difficulty. They often have to cope with major status changes in their lives at the time of leaving care: leaving foster care or their children's home and setting up a new home, and for some young people starting a family as well; leaving school and finding their way into further education, training or employment, or coping with unemployment.[32]

Fifth, as regards their lives after care, there is evidence that the Children (Leaving Care) Act 2000 (introduced in October 2001) has provided a stronger legal framework for care leavers than the earlier legislation.

In England, the proportion of young people leaving care at 18 is increasing. The new financial arrangements for 16- and 17-year-olds, including the use of incentive payments, have contributed to the increased participation of young people in further education and reduction in those not in education, employment and training.[33] There is also evidence of a strengthening of leaving care responsibilities, improved needs assessment, planning and the delivery of financial support, as well as improved levels of support by leaving care teams.[34]

What should be done?

In this context, improving outcomes for young people leaving care will require responses across the life course, as detailed below: encompassing the risks associated with their entry to care, their experiences in care, leaving care and their lives after care, to prevent their own children also being at risk of poverty.

- First of all, doing more to prevent young people coming into care. This will include reducing child poverty and providing support for parents and young people at home (as discussed elsewhere in this book).
- Improving the quality of care. This will include providing young people with stability and continuity in their lives while they are 'looked after', and improving their educational participation and achievement. Enhancing the career chances of care leavers needs to build upon the educational progress while young people are looked after. This is clearly recognised in the Social Exclusion Unit's report, *A Better Education for Children in Care*.[35] The need for five key changes is spelt out: greater stability; less time out of school; help with schoolwork; more help from home to support schoolwork; and improved health and well-being. There is research evidence that placement stability, positive encouragement, proactive placement, school and education service links, as well as compensatory assistance, can be helpful to young people.[36]
- Providing more gradual transitions. There is a marked contrast between the normative transitions of many young people and those leaving care. Why should we expect young people, whose lives have often been very difficult, to leave care at between 16 and 18 years of age? More gradual transitions, as is happening in some extended

foster care placements, will greatly assist these young people. The financial arrangements for post-18 funding are complex and clear guidance from local authorities to foster carers and young people will greatly assist this process.[37]

- The strengthening of the legal framework, as suggested above, has been positive. But there are still issues to be addressed.

The introduction of the Performance Assessment Framework provides essential official data for care leavers but this could be extended beyond 19, to reflect more normative transitions (eg, up to 25), as well as to include returns on different groups of care leavers: young black and minority ethnic care leavers; refugee and asylum seeking young people; young parents; young disabled people; young people with health problems, including mental health problems; and young offenders.

Regarding financial support, research has shown that the amount paid to most 'eligible' (16- and 17-year-olds still looked after) and 'relevant' (16- and 17-year-olds who have left care) young people is the same as the weekly state allowance paid to young people seeking work.[38] The same research reported that most local authorities (91 per cent) provided leaving care grants to 'relevant' and 'former relevant' (18–21-year-olds who have left care) young people to help them to live independently, and three-quarters provided financial incentives to encourage and sustain young people in education, employment and training. Education maintenance allowances provide an incentive as well as additional financial support for young people to continue in post-16 education.[39] Improvements could be made in three respects:

- Recognising the independent 'householder status' of 'relevant' and 'former relevant' care leavers by paying them the 'over 24' rate of benefit. The current system, in effect, condemns those young people living independently to poverty, as they are de facto householders but being paid at the same level as unemployed young people living at home.
- Allowing young people who have been in care to catch up with their education. This could be assisted by waiving the requirement that students of 18 and above claiming jobseeker's allowance and housing benefit, studying part time (16 hours or less a week), should have to give up their course if they are offered a job.
- Introducing transparent guidance and regulations for discretionary payments. There is currently considerable variation between local authorities, beyond individual need, in respect of leaving care grants, financial

assistance and financial incentives, especially for further and higher education. Such territorial injustices impact seriously upon the life chances of young people.

Finally, from April 2005, the introduction of the Child Trust Fund to parents of all children born after September 2002 provides an opportunity for local authorities to increase the financial assets of young people leaving care at 18. As a group, they are less likely than many of their peers to have their own assets, derived from family contributions. Both the Children Act 1989 ('local authorities must make such use of services for children cared for by their own parents') and the Children (Leaving Care) Act 2000 ('a duty to assist with the costs of education, employment and training') provide a statutory underpinning for making extra deposits into Child Trust Funds, linking this to financial advice as part of pathway planning, and providing assistance when the Trust reaches maturity.[40]

Conclusion

The main pathways to independence of care leavers predispose them to poverty. Since the introduction of the Children (Leaving Care) Act 2000 there is evidence of progress in three areas: young people leaving care later; improved qualifications; and improved participation in further education. But there is still a substantial gap between care leavers and other young people in respect of these and other areas. Improving the outcomes for young people leaving care, and thus reducing their routes into poverty, will require a more comprehensive series of measures directed at their life course, including their pre-care, in-care, leaving care and aftercare experiences. This should include:

- preventing young people entering care;
- improving the quality of care;
- ensuring opportunities for more normative and gradual transitions from care;
- extending and widening the Performance Assessment Framework for care leavers;
- recognising the 'householder status' of care leavers in benefit payments and the continuation of financial support for them to complete part-time education courses;

- introducing transparent guidance and regulations for discretionary financial assistance by local authorities;
- local authorities using the opportunities provided by the Child Trust Fund to increase the financial assets of young people leaving care at 18.

Notes

1 UN, *The UN Convention on the Rights of the Child*, United Nations, 1989

2 Department for Education and Skills, *Statistics of Education: care leavers, 2002–2003*, England, The Stationery Office, 2003, www.dfes.gov.uk/rsgateway/DB/SBU/b000423/index.shtml; Department for Education and Skills, *Children Looked After in England: 2002–03*, The Stationery Office, 2003; National Assembly for Wales, *Children Looked After by Local Authorities, 31 March 2003*, 2004, www.lgdu-wales.gov.uk/eng/pss.asp?cat=201&year =2003; Scottish Executive, *Children's Social Work Statistics 2002–03*, 2004, www.scotland.gov.uk/stats/bulletins/00287-00.asp; E Mooney, P McDowell and K Taggart, *Northern Ireland Care Leavers (2002/03)*, 2004, www.dhssp-sni.gov.uk/publications/2004/NI-CareLeavers-A4Pub.pdf

3 DfES, *Youth Cohort Study: the activities and experiences of 21 year olds: England and Wales 2000*, Department for Education and Skills, 2001

4 N Biehal, J Clayden, M Stein and J Wade, *Moving On: young people and leaving care schemes*, Her Majesty's Stationery Office, 1995; J Pinkerton and J McCrea, *Meeting the Challenge? Young people leaving care in Northern Ireland*, Ashgate, 1999; J Dixon and M Stein, *A Study of Throughcare and Aftercare Services in Scotland*, Scotland's Children, Children (Scotland) Act 1995, Research Findings No. 3, Scottish Executive, 2002; S Jackson, S Ajayi and M Quigley, *By Degrees: the first year, from care to university*, The Frank Buttle Trust, 2003; J Dixon, J Lee, J Wade, S Byford and H Weatherly, *Young People Leaving Care: an evaluation of costs and outcomes*, Report to the DfES, University of York, 2004

5 Department of Health, *Social Services Performance Indicators 2002–03*, Department of Health Publications, 2003

6 DfES, *Statistics of Education: outcome indicators for looked after children*, twelve months to 30 September 2003, England, Department for Education and Skills, 2004, www.dfes.gov.uk/rsgateway/DB/VOL/v000468/index.shtml

7 Social Exclusion Unit, *A Better Education for Children in Care*, The Stationery Office, 2003

8 N Biehal, J Clayden, M Stein and J Wade, *Moving On: young people and leaving care schemes*, Her Majesty's Stationery Office, 1995; B Broad, *Young People Leaving Care: life after the Children Act 1989*, Jessica Kingsley

Publishers, 1998; J Dixon and M Stein, *A Study of Throughcare and Aftercare Services in Scotland, Scotland's Children, Children (Scotland) Act 1995, Research Findings No. 3*, Scottish Executive, 2002; J Pinkerton and J McCrea, *Meeting the Challenge? Young people leaving care in Northern Ireland*, Ashgate, 1999

9 B Broad, *Improving the Health and Well Being of Young People Leaving Care*, Russell House Publishing, 2005

10 J Dixon, J Lee, J Wade, S Byford and H Weatherly, *Young People Leaving Care: an evaluation of costs and outcomes*, Report to the DfES, University of York, 2004

11 Department for Education and Skills, *Statistics of Education: care leavers, 2002–2003*, England, The Stationery Office, 2003, www.dfes.gov.uk/rsgate-way/DB/SBU/b000423/index.shtml

12 Department for Education and Skills, *Children in Need in England*, The Stationery Office, 2004, www.dfes.gov.uk/rsgateway/DB/VOL/v000451/index. shtml; National Assembly for Wales, *Children Looked After by Local Authorities, 31 March 2003*, 2004, www.lgdu-wales.gov.uk/eng/pss.asp?cat=201&year =2003; Scottish Executive, *Children's Social Work Statistics 2002–03*, 2004, www.scotland.gov.uk/stats/bulletins/00287-00.asp; E Mooney, P McDowell and K Taggart, *Northern Ireland Care Leavers (2002/03)*, 2004, www.dhssp-sni.gov.uk/publications/2004/NI-CareLeavers-A4Pub.pdf

13 J Dixon, J Lee, J Wade, S Byford and H Weatherly, *Young People Leaving Care: an evaluation of costs and outcomes*, Report to the DfES, University of York, 2004

14 G Jones, *The Youth Divide: diverging paths to adulthood*, Joseph Rowntree Foundation, 2002

15 J Dixon, J Lee, J Wade, S Byford and H Weatherly, *Young People Leaving Care: an evaluation of costs and outcomes*, Report to the DfES, University of York, 2004

16 M Stein, J Pinkerton and J Kelleher, 'Young people leaving care in England, Northern Ireland, and Ireland', *European Journal of Social Work,* 3:3, 2000, pp235–46

17 J Dixon and M Stein, *A Study of Throughcare and Aftercare Services in Scotland*, Scotland's Children, Children (Scotland) Act 1995, Research Findings No. 3, Scottish Executive, 2002

18 T Craig, *Off to a Bad Start*, Mental Health Foundation, 1996; Social Exclusion Unit, *Rough Sleeping*, The Stationery Office, 1998

19 Scottish Executive, *Children's Social Work Statistics 2002–03*, 2004, www.scotland.gov.uk/stats/bulletins/00287-00.asp

20 J Hobcraft and K Kiernan, *Childhood Poverty, Early Motherhood and Adult Social Exclusion*, CASE Paper 28, London School of Economics, 1999; Social Exclusion Unit, *Teenage Pregnancy*, The Stationery Office, 1999

21 N Biehal, J Clayden, M Stein and J Wade, *Moving On: young people and leaving care schemes*, Her Majesty's Stationery Office, 1995; J Pinkerton and J McCrea, *Meeting the Challenge? Young people leaving care in Northern Ireland*, Ashgate, 1999; J Dixon and M Stein, *A Study of Throughcare and Aftercare Services in Scotland, Scotland's Children, Children (Scotland) Act 1995, Research Findings No. 3*, Scottish Executive, 2002

22 National Statistics, *Households Below Average Income: an analysis of the income distribution 1994/5–2002/03*, DWP, 2004

23 J Hobcraft, *Intergenerational and Life-course Transmission of Social Exclusion: influences of childhood poverty, family disruption and contact with the police*, CASE Paper 15, London School of Economics, 1998

24 S Cheesbrough, *The Educational Attainment of People who have Been in Care: findings from the 1970 British cohort study*, 2002, www.socialexclusionunit. gov.uk

25 S Hutson, *Supported Housing: the experience of young care leavers*, Barnardo's, 1997; N Biehal and J Wade, 'Looking back, looking forward: care leavers, families and change', *Children and Youth Services Review*, 18:4/5, 1996, pp425–45

26 E Chase, A Knight, I Warwick and P Aggleton, *Pregnancy and Parenthood Among Young People In and Leaving Local Authority Care*, Report for the Department of Health, Thomas Coram Research Unit, 2003

27 R Lister, 'Citizenship on the margins: citizenship, social work and social action', *European Journal of Social Work*, 1, 1998, pp5–18; P Kemp, J Bradshaw, P Dornan, N Finch and E Mayhew, *Routes out of Poverty: a research review*, Joseph Rowntree Foundation, 2004

28 A Bebbington and J Miles, 'The background of children who enter local authority care', *British Journal of Social Work*, 19:5, 1989, pp349–86; Social Exclusion Unit, *A Better Education for Children in Care*, The Stationery Office, 2003

29 M Stein, 'Leaving care, education and career trajectories', *Oxford Review of Education,* 20:3, 1994, pp349–60

30 M Stein, *What Works for Young People Leaving Care?*, Barnardo's, 2004; M Stein and K Carey, *Leaving Care*, Blackwell, 1986

31 J Lakey, H Barnes and J Parry, *Getting a Chance: employment support for young people with multiple disadvantages*, Joseph Rowntree Foundation, 2001

32 M Stein, *What Works for Young People Leaving Care?*, Barnardo's, 2004

33 B Broad, *Improving the Health and Well Being of Young People Leaving Care*, Russell House Publishing, 2005; J Dixon, J Lee, J Wade, S Byford and H Weatherly, *Young People Leaving Care: an evaluation of costs and outcomes*, Report to the DfES, University of York, 2004

34 A S Allard, *A Case Study Investigation into the Implementation of the Children (Leaving Care) Act 2000*, NCH, 2002; N Hai and A Williams, *Implementing the Children (Leaving Care) Act 2000: the experience of eight London boroughs*, National Children's Bureau, London, 2004; B Broad, *Improving the Health and Well Being of Young People Leaving Care*, Russell House Publishing, 2005

35 Social Exclusion Unit, *A Better Education for Children in Care*, The Stationery Office, 2003

36 M Stein, 'Leaving care, education and career trajectories', *Oxford Review of Education,* 20:3, 1994, pp349–60; Social Exclusion Unit, *A Better Education for Children in Care*, The Stationery Office, 2003

37 Fostering Network, *Leaving Care and Foster Care, Financial Arrangements post 18*, 2005, www.fostering.net

38 B Broad, *Improving the Health and Well Being of Young People Leaving Care*, Russell House Publishing, 2005

39 J Dixon, J Lee, J Wade, S Byford and H Weatherly, *Young People Leaving Care: an evaluation of costs and outcomes*, Report to the DfES, University of York, 2004

40 D Maxwell, *Child Trust Funds and Local Authorities: challenges and opportunities*, Institute for Public Policy Research, 2004

Conclusion
Gabrielle Preston

Multiple disadvantages – making the links

As New Labour begins its third term in office, the children in this book continue to be disproportionately disadvantaged from the moment they are born. Indeed, all too often children's histories are written while they are still in the womb. Family income remains a major determinant of a child's health at birth, her/his educational attainment levels and the sort of job s/he is likely to get.

This will not come as a surprise to the Government. As discussed in the Introduction, it has become an expert analyst of poverty and social exclusion. However, although the Treasury's *Child Poverty Review* states that 'A child's life chances should not be determined by their parent's capacity to earn', the Social Exclusion Unit (SEU) accepts that:

> Children's life chances are still strongly affected by the circumstances of their parents. The social class a child is born into and their parents' level of education and health are still major determinants of their life chances and mean that social exclusion and disadvantage can pass from generation to generation.[1]

A number of overlapping themes emerge in *At Greatest Risk* – many of which have already been identified by the Government as a source of concern.[2] Issues around education, poor housing and employment are found in all the chapters. Ill health and disability – both a cause and a consequence of poverty – are prevalent among all the 'at risk' groups. For mothers, high levels of stress, anxiety and ill health may be exacerbated by judgemental, discriminatory or disjointed services. For some children, systems that have been put in place to redress inequalities – eg, within the education system – sometimes consolidate them. Community deprivation destroys childhood experiences and blights future prospects. Lone parenthood and ethnicity often compound underlying disadvantages. The focus on work as the primary – indeed, the only – route out of poverty has both marginalised and stigmatised families for whom it is not an option. Meanwhile, an inadequate and often inaccessible benefit system is failing to provide 'security for those who cannot work.'

Women, poverty, and family breakdown

Gender and lone parenthood arise as significant and cross cutting issues in this book. While lone parenthood is closely linked with living in poverty, poverty also puts relationships under considerable strain and can result in families breaking up. Although this may damage children's life chances, because of the association with an increased likelihood of poverty, some Government policies directly or indirectly contribute to the breakdown of families.

In her chapter on asylum seekers Pamela Fitzpatrick records how newborn babies are being taken into care because of a government policy that impoverishes asylum seeking mothers. Mike Stein reveals that many children are taken into care as a direct consequence of parental poverty. When a parent is in prison Jan Walker and Peter McCarthy report that, although maintaining family ties is vital in preventing reoffending and the risk of children learning offending behaviour, family breakdown is high. The link between disability and lone parenthood is also strong. Caring for a disabled partner or a child without adequate support places enormous strain on relationships.

Black and minority ethnic families

For a number of complex reasons, ethnicity often reinforces underlying disadvantages. Some black and minority ethnic (BME) families are more likely to be in the 'at risk' groups, to experience even greater disadvantages than white families within these 'at risk' groups, and are more likely to span different groups. For example, Gary Craig notes while only 8 per cent of white families and 29 per cent of Indian families contain five or more people, the figures rise to 59 and 65 per cent for Pakistani and Bangladeshi households. And Pamela Fitzpatrick reports:

A child aged between 5 and 9, in a two-parent household and whose parents were white owner-occupiers not dependent on social security benefits, had a 1 in 7,000 chance of entering care. A child of mixed race aged between 5 and 9 living in private rented accommodation with a lone parent who received income support had a 1 in 10 chance of entering care.

Poverty and ill health

The direct link between poverty and ill health or disability remains stubbornly in place. As Ruth Northway notes, childhood disability can arise from poor maternal nutrition, and 'children of parents in manual occupation groups have a higher risk of serious childhood illness and disability.' Parents of disabled children find that their own health suffers due to stress, which in turn has a negative impact on their employment opportunities.

Poverty is also linked with mental health problems which, the Government itself recognises, dramatically reduces opportunities to access employment and/or the benefit system. Sarah Cemlyn and Colin Clark report that Gypsies and Travellers have significantly poorer health than those of the same age, gender and economic status and are 'much more likely to experience anxiety, and, especially women, depression.' Pamela Fitzpatrick indicates that asylum seekers are 'vulnerable to … poor health, depression, loneliness, stress and family breakdown.' Young children of asylum seekers in the UK experience particular health problems such as weight loss, mouth infections, persistent respiratory conditions, skin complaints and 'a general failure to thrive'.

Sue Regan and Jenny Neuberger note that inadequate housing also contributes to underlying health problems, including 'both the development of mental health problems, such as depression, and physical health problems, such as asthma caused by damp and condensation.'

The political context and structural problems

A number of the issues raised in this book relate directly to the Government's strategy on child poverty. These are discussed below.

Rights and responsibilities

The Government is very keen on rights and responsibilities, and yet some children – for example, Gypsies and Travellers, and those who have a parent in prison – are not accorded the rights that childhood should bring. Despite the fact that the UK is a signatory to the UN Convention on the Rights of the Child and the Government itself has identified many of the children in this book as being at particular risk,[3] some of Britain's most vulnerable children are neither seen nor heard. Most disturbing of all, some aspects of legislation actively undermine children's status as children. Pamela Fitzpatrick notes that for the children of asylum seekers, 'their status of asylum seekers is given precedence over their status as children'. This is in direct contravention of Article 16[4] and Article 22[5] of the UN Convention on the Rights of the Child.

Other children register in the public consciousness only when they are perceived as being part of a vilified group. 'Blame and shame' is an integral part of the nation's psyche, although it is a culture which detracts from the Government's agenda on poverty and society inclusion. Misguided and sometimes inflammatory ministerial rhetoric around respect and discipline, and the compulsion to demonise some children as 'yobs' is a source of mounting concern. Slapping anti-social behaviour orders, curfews and custodial sentences on children who are already at risk[6] flies in the face of the Government's *Every Child Matters* agenda. It is to be hoped that the Government's eagerly awaited Green Paper on youth[7] will inculcate a more positive and understanding approach to young people. However, for the moment, young people seem to get significantly more stick than carrot.

Many of the young people in this book are affected by a judgemental rather than a supportive approach. Jan Walker and Peter McCarthy comment that parental imprisonment has a direct impact upon children who 'feel let down and experience emotional and behavioural problems.' However, they emphasise that rather than receiving support, children are themselves 'labelled as deviant and excluded even further'.

Their parents fare no better. Although many of this book's contributors emphasise that parenting is significantly harder when money, status and self esteem are in short supply, the Government seems intent on reflecting and reinforcing the media's and the public's compulsion to demonise and judge parents who are struggling to cope. As Pamela Fitzpatrick points out in relation to asylum seekers, being forced to leave their home, give up their career, family and friends, and often suffer severe trauma 'may well affect their ability to care for their children'. Nevertheless, support and understanding is in very short supply. Harsh solutions do little to relieve problems of poverty – indeed, they often compound them. Drawing on research which has found evidence of a link between crime and poverty, Jan Walker and Peter McCarthy emphasise that 'Sending a parent to prison provides a marker for a range of linked effects, all of which contribute to and reinforce the propensity for child poverty', yet custodial sentences are on the increase.

This book clearly reveals that punishing parental behaviours – or penalising them because of their national or ethnic status, or because they are unable or unwilling to work – is not only unjust for the parent, but it means punishing children for something they haven't done. Although the *Child Poverty Review* promises to support and protect children 'so they do not suffer as a result of their parents' circumstances',[8] all too often – as Jan Walker and Peter McCarthy point out – children are the 'indisputably innocent victims'.

Work – a route out of poverty?

Accessing paid employment plays a crucial role in the Government's strategy for the eradication of child poverty. The seemingly intractable link between worklessness and poverty clearly suggests that, for most families, sustainable, well paid employment is the *only* viable route out of poverty. However, work is not a reliable route out of poverty for everybody. For many of the families in this book, barriers to employment, low pay and living in single earner households significantly reduces the ability of employment to draw them out of poverty.

Low levels of educational achievement, poor training, ill health or discrimination, along with structural problems such as inadequate childcare or a lack of appropriate and/or locally accessible jobs, mean that even when families do access paid employment it is often, as David Piachaud points out, 'insecure and poorly rewarded'. Furthermore, despite a number of Government initiatives aimed at drawing low income families into paid employment – including New Deals, Pathways to Work, and legislation designed to reduce discrimination – many families in this book continue to face almost insurmountable barriers to the labour market. For example, Gary Craig reports that 'racism in the selection of people for jobs or redundancy and the greater likelihood of being in low-paid work' renders employment an unreliable route out of poverty for some minority ethnic communities.

Families with disabled children also face significant barriers to employment.[9] For the minority who do access paid employment, it may not be financially beneficial. Ruth Northway emphasises that families with disabled children spend significantly longer periods of time caring for their children. As a consequence, when they return to work 'they may find themselves offered work which is low paid and often below their level of training/qualifications'.

The Government acknowledges that 'Disabled people often experience multiple forms of labour market disadvantage.'[10] However, while Hugh Stickland and Richard Olsen argue that more should be done to improve employment opportunities for disabled parents, they note that when they do move into work 'the risk of poverty is greater for children with disabled parents than those with non-disabled parents.' They attribute this to the likelihood of disabled people being in relatively low paid, part-time and insecure work.

Larger families – who often span the 'at risk' groups – also face additional barriers to paid employment. Jonathan Bradshaw observes that apart from the desire to spend time with their children, having to arrange and co-ordinate childcare can be a deterrent to mothers taking on paid work. He also emphasises that larger families who do work are likely to be poorer than smaller families, because pay packets do not recognise additional family needs.

Furthermore, work is not a route out of poverty for families who are actively excluded from labour market participation – such as asylum seekers.

Security for those who cannot work?

Given the difficulties mentioned above, it is essential that the benefit system provides an adequate financial safety net to safeguard families from poverty. But is financial security being provided for those who cannot work? New Labour has introduced substantial improvements to benefits for children (see p20). However, high levels of poverty in workless families raise serious questions about the structural effectiveness and administrative reliability, the adequacy and the accessibility of the benefit system.

Children in the 'at risk' groups are disproportionately reliant on benefits that, as Sue Middleton reports, remain woefully inadequate. The adult rate of income support (IS) comes in for a great deal of criticism. As David

Piachaud points out, 'the "safety net" provided by the State is still far below its own poverty level', a situation he angrily denounces as 'inconsistent, indefensible and shameful.'

Paul Dornan points out that keeping adult IS levels so low saps improvements in financial support targeted at children and undermines progress on the eradication of child poverty. Recipients of IS live a hand to mouth existence which not only generates high levels of stress and ill health – thereby reducing the possibility of being able to work – but throws the veracity of the Government's claim to provide security for those who cannot work into serious doubt.

Furthermore, a number of contributors highlight the fact that lack of information and an increasingly complex system exclude some of the UK's most vulnerable citizens from accessing the benefits to which they are entitled. Gary Craig indicates that, for families from BME communities in the UK, take-up of benefits is lower than for the white population because of 'confusion about the system, cultural obstacles and the failure of the social security system to provide adequate help for minorities seeking access to benefits.' Sarah Cemlyn and Colin Clark also note that Travellers and Gypsies face 'discrimination and disadvantage in accessing the benefit system'.

A complex system often prevents disabled parents and disabled children accessing the benefits to which they are entitled. Hugh Stickland and Richard Olsen note that, while disability benefits do safeguard some families from poverty, many – often lone parents – do not claim the incapacity benefits to which they are entitled. Despite the fact that families with disabled children incur additional costs, Ruth Northway records that often they 'do not receive the level of benefits to which they are entitled due to a lack of information concerning such benefits and difficulties with making applications.' The Government accepts that 'Families from BME groups with disabled children have a lower take-up of services, and often feel less informed or able to access the system.'[11]

Most iniquitous of all is the treatment of asylum seekers. Pamela Fitzpatrick reports:

> ...they cannot work or claim social security benefits, have no access to permanent housing, and at best receive support that is set well below subsistence level by way of a largely unregulated parallel benefit system.

'Security for those who cannot work' is, for the moment, more aspirational rhetoric than reality for many of the families in this book.

Social exclusion

In the words of the SEU:

> Social exclusion is about more than income poverty. It is a shorthand term for what can happen when people or areas face a combination of linked problems such as unemployment, discrimination, poor skills, low income, poor housing, high crime, bad health and family breakdown ... (it) is an extreme consequence of what happens when people don't get a fair deal throughout their lives, often because of the disadvantage they face at birth.[12]

Despite this welcome and insightful analysis, a worrying theme that emerges from this book is that Government policy is not only proving largely irrelevant for some of the UK's most disadvantaged children, in some cases it is actively making the situation worse. Sarah Cemlyn and Colin Clark point out that the exclusion experienced by Gypsies and Travellers has been compounded by the '*substantive* denial of ethnic minority status and corresponding rights.' Jan Walker and Peter McCarthy state that:

> Social inclusion – the realisation of citizenship economically and socially – militates against crime. Conversely, social exclusion – homelessness, worklessness and social alienation – creates the desperation which frequently gives rise to criminal activities.

Most shocking of all, as governments have sought to prove their toughness on immigration issues, successive legislation has led to the active economic and social exclusion of asylum seekers. This flies in the face of Government policy on poverty which, as Pamela Fitzpatrick observes, 'is about social inclusion and non-discrimination ... Yet ... asylum policy is about non-integration, about separateness and otherness.'

Educational disadvantages

The Government – rightly – looks to the education system to redress some of the inequalities that beset children's lives. However, this book suggests that far from compensating disadvantaged children, the educational system may compound difficulties.

The causes of educational underachievement among children at risk of poverty are complex. Gary Craig writes that it is not simply to do with the relationship between poverty and educational disadvantage, but with the education system itself. He points out that, although educational achievement among minority ethnic groups is variable, most BME children encounter disadvantage and discrimination within the system from a very early age.

The impact of poor educational achievement is costly for individuals and society alike. In the case of prisoners, Jan Walker and Peter McCarthy write that, compared to non-offenders, they are 'more likely...to have received a poor education,...truanted or been excluded from school.' Sarah Cemlyn and Colin Clark report that Gypsy and Traveller children have been identified as the 'group most at risk in the education system.'

Other groups are also disadvantaged. Mike Stein notes that young people leaving care are particularly poorly served by the education system, experiencing lower levels of educational attainment at 16 and 18 and lower post-16 participation rates than their peer group. All too often, poor educational progress is compounded by restricted training and labour market opportunities. Mike Stein reports that care leavers are also less likely to be engaged in post-16 education, employment and training than other young people aged between 16 and 19 in the population.

As with so many other areas discussed in this book, the children of asylum seekers are treated quite differently from other children. Notions of integration, mainstreaming and the importance of educating disadvantaged children in a mixed environment[13] are seemingly irrelevant for these most vulnerable of children. Pamela Fitzpatrick notes that the intention of the The Nationality, Immigration and Asylum Act 2002 was 'that children would be removed from mainstream education and instead educated separately with other asylum seekers.'

Social care

Despite the Government's attempts to co-ordinate and integrate children's services, disjointed and inappropriate service provision often adds to families' difficulties. Gary Craig discusses the multiple ways in which BME ethnic families are disadvantaged, and reports that social care provision 'remains fairly uneven at best'. Sarah Cemlyn and Colin Clark observe how 'vulnerable Gypsy and Traveller children may be ignored because they do not fit mainstream systems'. Pamela Fitzpatrick points out that local authorities are actively prevented from providing support to failed asylum seekers.

As discussed above, the focus on the parent often displaces considerations of the needs of the child. Jan Walker and Peter McCarthy observe that:

> In assessing risk factors for children, there has been a tendency to focus on the parental offending behaviour and to ignore the complex repercussions of imprisonment...Any help that is available at present tends to be provided by different agencies addressing different problems, with little evidence of joined-up service provision.

Housing

For many of the children in this book, inadequate housing, living in temporary accommodation or homelessness compound and consolidate disadvantages in a variety of inter-linking ways. Sue Regan and Jenny Neuberger report that 'BME households are more than six times more likely than white households to be overcrowded...[or] homeless and living in temporary accommodation...' and that children who have disabilities or chronic health problems are put at greater risk by poor housing conditions and inadequate access to services. They highlight the fact that poor housing is not only distressing and damaging in its own right, but it disrupts access to schools and the labour market, and erodes social and support networks. It damages the health of parents and children, and tears families apart.

Sara Cemlyn and Colin Clark indicate that when Gypsies and Travellers are 'pushed' into housing, they experience 'poor conditions; overcrowding, often temporary housing; and also problems of stress because housing is culturally alien...' Children leaving care are also at particular risk, as are asylum seekers.

Recommendations

Unravelling the causes and the consequences of poverty is clearly a complex enterprise. However, this book raises a number of issues that need to be addressed, and they are outlined below. These reflect, reiterate and reinforce the demands outlined in CPAG's manifesto, *Ten steps to a society free of child poverty*.[14]

The role of paid work

If employment provides 'opportunity and security',[15] then it is right and proper for paid work to play a central role in the Government's strategy on the eradication of child poverty. However, while people who are able and willing to take up paid work should be assisted to do so, 'welfare to work' is not necessarily an appropriate or an effective strategy for the families in this book. Forcing people into jobs that may be low paid and insecure will not reduce child poverty. Apart from the fact that around half of currently income poor children have one or more parent in work, low wages may generate or exacerbate health problems, stress, or depression – major causes of people moving *out* of employment. Furthermore, the emphasis on drawing parents who have experienced multiple disadvantages from the word go into employment that is unlikely to prove either well paid or rewarding, may well sabotage Government attempts to break cycles of disadvantage for their children. CPAG urges the Government to review its welfare to work strategy in the light of the following issues. First, not all adults can work. Even if an 80 per cent employment target is reached, one in five will not be in paid employment. Second, wages do not cater for the additional spending needs that arise from having children, or the extra costs incurred by some families. And third, not all parents can command the same wages, perhaps because of caring responsibilities, lack of skills or discrimination.

CPAG urges the Government to:

- increase wages for the poorest earners. The minimum wage must go up in real terms – above the rate of earnings inflation;
- work towards better jobs, not just more jobs;
- increase efforts to enhance adult skills.

Education and training

It is a sad fact of life that children who are born into low income families do less well out of the 'free' British state educational system than their better-off peers. Children who need to do better than their peer group to compensate them for a disadvantaged start in life are doing worse.[16] Although the causes of educational disadvantage are complex, many of the difficulties experienced by children are a direct consequence of their parents' income levels – which, in turn, is heavily influenced by parental educational qualifications. It is to be hoped that the Government's various initiatives to improve early childhood experiences and educational attainment levels will draw dividends in both the short term – by improving childhood experiences – and in the long term – by enhancing these children's prospects of accessing financially rewarding and sustainable jobs if they can work, and facilitating a fulfilling and secure existence if they cannot. However, this will not happen unless their parents are also drawn out of poverty.

CPAG urges the Government to:

- maximise life chances by ensuring that policies take account of the many ways in which poverty restricts poorer children's ability to join in and participate fully in school life;
- ensure all children have full access to the requirements – meals, uniforms and activities – of their education;
- weight educational funding in favour of the early years – when all children will benefit and it is most effective.

Security for those who cannot work

'Security for those who cannot work' is being undermined by a number of factors. An increasingly complex and often impenetrable benefit and tax credit system is disempowering recipients and generating administrative problems. Where support is available it does make a real difference, for example in households with a disabled child or adult. However, families who are in greatest need are the least likely to access the benefits to which they are entitled.

Since many of the children discussed in this book are disproportionately reliant upon key safety net benefits (IS, child tax credit (CTC) and child benefit), addressing adequacy is critical to improving their life chances. To safeguard children from living in poverty, all children (including the children of asylum seekers) must be caught by a comprehensive financial safety net. This bedrock of provision requires effective benefit and tax credit administrative processes which ensure that all families receive their full benefit entitlement and avoid 'cliff edges' in family incomes due to the sudden withdrawal of benefits or the recovery of overpaid benefits or tax credits.

In addition to an effective safety net, the benefit and tax credit system must meet additional needs, for example by increasing disability living allowance, or by increasing and reversing the current weighting of child benefit (which favours smaller families), or by providing additional support via the per child element of CTC.

CPAG urges the Government to:

- uprate the combined value of child tax credit and child benefit at least in line with the fastest growing of either prices or earnings. The element of this that is child benefit ought to be maximised;
- increase the adult payments within income support in line with those for children;
- reform the administration of tax credits and benefits – ensure they provide the right amount to the right people at the right time;
- provide benefit entitlement to all UK residents equally, irrespective of their immigration status;
- establish a Minimum Income Standards Commission which is independent of, but funded by, government and responsible to Parliament, to review evidence and conduct research on the adequacy of benefits and tax credits.

Service provision

The Government Green Paper, *Every Child Matters*, aims to ensure that all children and young people are healthy, stay safe, enjoy and achieve, make a positive contribution, and achieve economic well-being. Unfortunately, many of the children in this book are barred from these fundamental rights. Clearly, more needs to be done to improve the quality, delivery and accessibility of services – particularly childcare, education, health, social services and transport.

CPAG urges the Government to:

- deliver services that recognise children first and foremost as children, not as asylum seekers or any other group;
- provide high quality services to all children, irrespective of their parent's national, ethnic or work status.

A final message to Government

1. **Language**: Although, as this book demonstrates, New Labour has mastered the language of disadvantage and social exclusion, all too often different elements within the Government sabotage insightful social analysis by utilising inflammatory and discriminatory language. Misguided rhetoric on asylum seekers and attempts to 'get tough' with lone parents or disabled adults – whom the Government wishes to encourage into paid employment – sends out confusing and, as this book demonstrates, negative, unjust and largely self-defeating messages.

2. **Statistics**: Given the statistical shortcomings discussed in the Introduction, the authors in this book have had to make the best of often inadequate data. This highlights the difficulty of analysing the impact of Government policy on the most disadvantaged people. The Government must ensure that better data is compiled on groups facing particular risks and the overlaps between these groups.

3. **Poverty proof policies**: The root cause of child poverty is inadequate income. Its consequences are complex and wide-ranging. These cut across many boundaries of governmental responsibility. The Government recognises the need for joined-up solutions.[17] However, this book confirms that not only are some government departments failing to focus directly on the goal of tackling child poverty, but they may be pursuing policies which actually worsen the situation for families who are at greatest risk. If child poverty is to be eradicated, poverty proofing of policies must be applied to all relevant departments, not just the Treasury or the DWP. This would ensure that policy interventions and spending priorities support and enhance, rather than undermine, the achievement of the child poverty ambition.

Notes

1 Social Exclusion Unit, *Breaking the Cycle: taking stock of progress and priorities for the future*, Office of the Deputy Prime Minister, 2004, p10

2 Ibid. 'The main causes and consequences of social exclusion are: low income; unemployment; poor educational attainment; poor mental or physical health; family breakdown and poor parenting; poor housing and homelessness; discrimination; crime; living in a disadvantaged area', p7

3 In *Breaking the Cycle: taking stock of progress and priorities for the future*, Office of the Deputy Prime Minister, 2004, the Social Exclusion Unit identified the following groups as a major priorities: people with physical or mental health problems; those who lack skills or qualifications, both formal qualifications and broader basic life skills; people from some ethnic minority groups, including asylum seekers and refugees, p11

4 'No child should be subjected to arbitrary or unlawful interference with his or her privacy, family, home or correspondence, nor to unlawful attacks on his or her honour and reputation' and 'The child has the right to the protection of the law against such interference and attacks'.

5 '…a child who is seeking refugee status or who is considered a refugee…shall, whether unaccompanied or accompanied by his or her parents or by any other person, receive appropriate protection and humanitarian assistance in the enjoyment of applicable rights set forth in the present Convention and in all other international human rights or humanitarian instruments to which the said States are Parties.'

6 See, for example, M Bright, 'Children with autism the target of Asbos', *The Observer*, 22 May 2005

7 This much delayed Green Paper, now scheduled to be published in summer 2005, will focus on 'places to go, things to do', vulnerability, and support, advice and guidance.

8 HM Treasury, *Child Poverty Review*, The Stationery Office, 2004, p16

9 Ibid. Only 3% of mothers with disabled children are in full time employment (compared with 22% of mothers with non-disabled children) and only 13% manage part-time work (compared with 39% of mothers with non-disabled children), p22.

10 'More than 40% of disabled people are low skilled; around 25% of disabled people of working age are over 50 years; around 10% are from BME groups.' Prime Minister's Strategy Unit, *Improving the Life Chances of Disabled People. Final Report*, Prime Minister's Strategy Unit, 2005, p6

11 Ibid., p33

12 Social Exclusion Unit, *Breaking the Cycle: taking stock of progress and priorities for the future*, Office of the Deputy Prime Minister, 2004, p17

13 'Children from disadvantaged backgrounds benefit particularly from care in groups made up of a wide ragne of children, suggesting there are social gains from ensuring that children attending a group setting come from a range of backgrounds,' HM Treasury, *Choice for Parents, the Best Start for Children: a ten year strategy for childcare*, HMSO, 2004, p14

14 CPAG's manifesto, *Ten Steps to a Society Free of Child Poverty*, CPAG, 2005

15 HM Government, *Department for Work and Pensions Five Year Strategy: opportunity and security throughout life*, Department for Work and Pensions, 2005

16 Research from the Sutton Trust and the London School of Economics and Political Science reveal that social mobility in Britain is lower than in other advanced countries and declining. They conclude that 'the strength of the relationship between educational attainment and family income, especially for access to higher education, is at the heart of Britain's low mobility culture and what sets us apart from other European and North American countries.' See J Blanden, P Gregg and S Machin, *Intergenerational Mobility in Europe and North America*, a report supported by the Sutton Trust, Centre for Economic Performance, London School of Economics and Political Science, 2005

17 See HM Treasury, *The Child Poverty Review*, The Stationery Office, 2004; 'Making further progress requires cross-Government action,' p85